THE NEW ELECTRIC BALLROOM

The power of storytelling and the mythology of everyday life combine in this play set in a small fishing village in the west of Ireland, where, night after night, two aging sisters reenact an evening in the early '60s at the New Electric Ballroom.

The New Electric Ballroom, a companion piece to *The Walworth Farce*, was first produced in English by The Druid Theatre in Galway. In 2008, it won the Edinburgh Fringe First Award and received its U.S. premiere at St. Ann's Warehouse in 2009 in Brooklyn.

ENDA WALSH is a Dublin born playwright who now lives in London. His plays have been translated into twenty languages. Among his best known plays are *Disco Pigs* and *Bedbound*. He has received two Edinburgh Fringe First awards in consecutive years for *The Walworth Farce* and *The New Electric Ballroom*. He wrote the screenplay for *Hunger* (2008), the story of the final days of IRA hunger striker Bobby Sands, which won numerous awards, including the Camera d'Or at the Cannes Film Festival.

THE NEW ELECTRIC BALLROOM

THE NEW ELECTRIC BALLROOM

Enda Walsh

THEATRE COMMUNICATIONS GROUP
NEW YORK
2009

The Walworth Farce and *The New Electric Ballroom* is published by Theatre Communications Group, Inc., 520 Eighth Avenue, 24th Floor, New York, NY 10018-4156, by special arrangement with Nick Hern Books Limited.

The Walworth Farce and *The New Electric Ballroom* were first published in Great Britain by Nick Hern Books Limited in association with the Druid Theatre Company.

A CIP catalog record for this book is available from the Library of Congress.

ISBN-13: 978-1-55936-354-9

Cover photos: George Marks, Hulton Archive/Getty Images (Ballroom); Three Lions, Hulton Archive/Getty Images (Walworth).

Cover design by John Gall

First TCG Edition, October 2009

To Jo Ellison

Characters

BREDA, *sixties*

CLARA, *sixties*

ADA, *forty*

PATSY, *a fishmonger*

This text went to press before the end of rehearsals and so may differ slightly from the play as performed.

A living room/kitchen space.

On a wall, three different sets of clothes hanging on separate hangers. A cashmere jumper and a rara skirt; a 1950's red blouse and a blue pleated skirt; and a glitzy show-business man's suit.

A small kitchen counter with a large delicious-looking sponge cake on it.

The atmosphere immediately taut and aggressive.

Two older women, in their sixties, BREDA *and* CLARA, *and a younger one,* ADA, *who is forty.*

CLARA *is sitting.* BREDA *is standing in the corner facing the wall.* ADA *is standing right behind her, staring intently at the back of her head.* ADA *slightly out of breath. She's holding some lipstick in her hand.*

BREDA (*fast and frightened*). By their nature people are talkers. You can't deny that. You could but you'd be affirming what you're trying to argue against and what would the point of that be? No point. Just adding to the sea of words that already exist out there in your effort to say that people are not talkers. But people talk and no one in their right mind would challenge that. Unless you're one of those poor souls starved of vocal cords or that Willy Prendergast boy who used live in town and only managed three words. One was 'yes', one was 'no' and one was 'fish'. Yes yes yes. No no no. Fish fish fish. Fish yes yes. Fish no no. Yes no fish. No yes fish. Fish no fish. Fish yes fish. So even he talked.

CLARA. Look at my little feet.

BREDA. People are born talkers. Those present when a baby comes into the world are made all too aware that the womb is a more desirable place for a baby. That and the unglamorous entrance the baby must make. For all his miracles and great creations, you'd imagine our Lord could have created a more dignified point of arrival. This is the man who did wonders with the mouth and ears and surpassed Himself with the eyes but sharing a channel with the 'waterworks department' doesn't strike me as the healthiest environment for a yet-to-be-born baby and I'm not even a plumber.

CLARA. Would you look at these tiny little hands!

BREDA. People talking just for the act of it. Words spinning to nothing. For no definable reason. Like a little puppy, a hungry puppy yapping for his supper, yap-yap-yap-yap… that's people with words. The breath and the word are interchangeable. Interchangeable!? Identical. Of course people breathe to live. While they talk to…

CLARA. I'm getting smaller! I worry too much. Worry does that, Ada. It does! It stunts you, does worry! Look at the size of me in this chair. Like a midget!

ADA. You're not a midget.

CLARA. A cup of tea, a cup of tea will sort me out.

BREDA. Won't make you any taller.

CLARA (*snaps*). There's nothing I can't see from here, bitch!

ADA. How could you know that?

CLARA. Instinct.

ADA. Christ…

CLARA. Aren't we ever going to have tea again? Where's my tea?

ADA (*mimicking*). 'Where's my tea? Where's my tea?'

CLARA. Fetch me my tea, 'Breda the bad girl'.

ADA. There'll be no tea today. (*Turns back and snaps.*) Breda!

BREDA. For that's people with their great need to talk. The terrible necessity of it. And even besides the talking, far deeper than the talking, is this need to connect somehow. To belong. We're out into the world and all is noise and light and we're speaking of the womb being a more desirable place and it's like the nurse has given us a pill.

CLARA (*mumbles longingly*). Oh, what chance a pill?

BREDA. And the pill gives us this need to belong to 'mother', to 'father', to 'brothers and sisters' and 'in-laws' and 'friends' and 'strangers about to be friends' and 'strangers who'll always be strangers'. The talking is important but superficial really, 'cause the pill gives us a greater compulsion to connect with all these people. To be a part.

CLARA. Fish fish fish! Fish yes fish. No yes fish!

BREDA. But here's the thing…

ADA. Turn around now.

> BREDA *stops and turns around from the corner and faces* ADA. *Her face is aggressively marked with red lipstick, we guess that it's been done by* ADA. BREDA *holds a ceramic kitchen bowl. Seeing her,* CLARA, *frightened, covers her eyes.*

> (*Quietly prompting.*) Wherever…

> *A slight pause.*

BREDA. Wherever that pill resides in the body it doesn't reach the further recesses of the brain. 'Cause sitting back there… back there and likely only to make the odd appearance, is the 'hard truth'…

ADA. Slow.

> *A pause.*

BREDA (*slower*). And the 'hard truth' reminds us that we'll always be alone, baby sister. Besides the yap-yap and the arms outstretched and our great compulsion to be with others, we'll always be back in the womb. Back there and reminding ourselves that the womb is a more desirable place than this 'created world'. We don't want to be alone but we're alone. We don't want to be an island but we are that island.

A pause.

Will I put the piece of paper back in its bowl, Ada?

She does so and ADA *takes the bowl off her.*

ADA (*to* BREDA). Is it true we're alone?

BREDA *nods.*

Us more than anyone else?

BREDA. The same.

BREDA *touches her nose. Blood spills down her face.* ADA *just looks at her.*

CLARA (*announcing*). Nobody… Makes… Cake… Like… You… Clara.

BREDA *goes to sit down.*

Our mother would always say that. She said I was a born baker. She said I had a gift for coffee cake the way Jesus had a gift for sacrifice. When I was six she'd place me on her lap and I'd mix the flour with the eggs and the sugar and the coffee. And we'd be half-listening to the radio and her leg would send me up and down like I'm on a horse trotting. Not galloping now! Never a gallop. She'd get me to recite the alphabet while the cake stretched out in the heat inside. The lovely pattern of the ABCs over and over as it pumps the air into the sponge. Me and the oven in happy unison, in lovely poetry. Sure, look at the consistency of that sponge cake!

BREDA. Enough, Clara!

BREDA *stares over at* ADA *who is lost in her thoughts.* BREDA *starts removing the lipstick from her face with some baby wipes.*

CLARA. If it was entered into a contest… imagine the envy. Imagine all those old bitches hiding their hate because of my prize. A local photographer is there and their faces looking up at me, Ada. The girls from the cannery looking at me! At me! And I turn to Holy Mary, 'cause she's standing there right beside, and the mother of Jesus takes me aside and says, 'You're the best, Clara. Better than all them who locked you inside. Who spun out the gossip in the cannery and locked that door behind you. You're better than all those bitches.'

BREDA. Clara!

CLARA. So I slice off a piece of cake for the mother of Jesus… and she scoffs it down, not in the least bit like a virgin, but what do you expect, what with the great divinity of this sponge? What colour rosette would they give me for winning with such a great coffee cake? There's too many colours to choose from. What heavenly colour, Ada?

A very long pause.

There's a terrible lull in the conversation. The sort of lull that can get you worrying about other things.

A pause.

Will I take the piece of paper from the bowl, Ada?

ADA *doesn't answer.*

Can we not have a cup of tea and some of that lovely coffee cake I made?

A pause.

BREDA (*to* ADA). Did something happen outside, pet?

A long pause.

ADA. The town still asleep I cycle to work as always. Through the little narrow streets and over the cobble-stones away from the sea and towards the cannery up on the hill. I see a furniture van outside Mrs Cullen's house.

She's getting a new kitchen put in and her stood watching the men carrying the fancy cabinets through her garden and into her house. Her little dog Bobby's bouncing up and down and yapping the way little dogs do. I can see her looking at me as I pass by and a coldness in her face because of what us three are to them. I cycle on and into the cannery and walk through the floor with the loud machines tinning the fish... still echoing with the gossip of Clara and Breda and the Roller Royle. Into my little office and head down and lost in the numbers and turning fish into money. Just me and the machines. No one but me and the sea being tinned. (*Slight pause*.) It's evening and I cycle home and the streets are again empty and that furniture van passes and gets me thinking of Mrs Cullen's new fitted kitchen and for some reason I stop my bike outside her house. And I'm standing there imagining her in a yellow light surrounded by all her new things. (*Pause*.) He's lying on the ground dying. His insides are more out than in. His blond hair stuck with blood and bits. I can see the whole scene played out. The kitchen fitted and Mrs Cullen inside and Bobby bouncing up and down and yapping at the men as they get into the van. And the van pulls away and Bobby closer and closer still and caught under the wheel and laid into the road. I'm seeing all of this played out with Mrs Cullen at her door and walking towards me and then seeing Bobby lying on the road and then bent over getting sick into her begonias... and she's crying now... she's crying. (*Pause*.) I'm standing with my bicycle watching and...!! I start to smile. I'm smiling at a woman and her dying dog. (*Slight pause*.) How is it I've come to feel this way?

A door opens. It's PATSY *the fishmonger with a plastic tray full of large fish.*

PATSY. All right, the ladies?

BREDA. Leave them where you stand and go.

PATSY *puts down the tray.*

PATSY. Terrific news about Nana Cotter, isn't it? A hundred years, God bless her, and a lovely letter from the President of congratulations.

A pause as the sisters don't answer.

To mark the occasion she got her hair done in a purple rinse and a party was thrown with all manner of vol-au-vents and trifle present.

A pause as the sisters remain silent.

Poor love got a little excited and shit herself...

CLARA. Would you look at these tiny little feet!

PATSY. Yeah, she's a great woman, Nana, all right. Little bones like summer kindling, hands like pigeon's feet, hearing shot from years of working in the cannery but by Jesus can she eat trifle? Eat it? Like a Hoover!

A pause. He doesn't want to leave, despite it being obvious he's an unwelcome guest.

Mr Simmons got his hip done. Looks a hell of lot more normal than before. Great to see him back all level. He's a sprightly ninety-year-old, despite all his misfortunes. Feck it, he's had that many trips to the garage, he's more plastic than flesh, but to see his little cataract eyes lit up with renewed life...

BREDA. You can go now, we're busy.

PATSY. But what a lovely smell of coffee cake in here. Different houses have their own stamp. I could close my eyes and still make my way around town if the front doors were open. I'd be the first to say I'm not the sharpest knife in the rack and I'm no looker either. People have said I have the looks of a man who's been struck in the face by a wet fish and I couldn't argue with that for the truth is I have often been struck by a wet fish in the face. Several times in fact. But when it comes to smelling things... well, boys!! You won't find a keener nose in the whole of the county! Obviously some people think that's an unfortunate ability, what with me being a fishmonger, and they wouldn't be wrong...

CLARA (*blocks her ears and mumbles*). Yes no no! No yes fish! Fish fish fish...

PATSY. But God, that was a great night the other night! Mags Donald had all her grandchildren in the pub and while I was only passing through to use the gents I had to stop a while and listen to the great sing-along. Like a lark her little crippled grandson sang and we were all reduced to tears when Mags got up and said what a gift from God this little spastic was. But feck it, what breeding! Like their own village they were. Masses of them spread around her feet like Mags herself was giving a sermon at the Mount and though no loaves and fishes were present there was plenty of crisps and scampi...

BREDA (*snaps*). What is it, Patsy!?

A pause. Again he looks towards the open door and then back.

PATSY. Things are odd. (*Slight pause.*) Outside.

BREDA. Tell him stop, Ada!

ADA *lowers her head.*

Leave!

PATSY. I'm standing in the little shoebox I call my bedroom, Ada. I'm standing in my underpants. I'm standing there staring down on my little bed, the sheets all creased and...? Like skin. The pillow dented from where I lay my head. The shape of me marked out on the bed, mapping out my night's sleep. And for some reason that gets me nervous so that I have to leave the room. The house quiet as always. The little stairs groaning as always. Everything as always but for this ball of butterflies growing inside me. So I dress real quick and leave and off and out to work. I'm outside then. And the narrow cobbled streets of the town are a bit uneasy underfoot. The narrow streets narrower somehow.

The houses on either side, they're leaning in that bit close to me. They're squeezing me, hurrying me towards work. I come to the little harbour to gather up my fish from the boats like I always do. I say hello to Simple Paddy who helps out in the harbour tying up the boats. I listen to his dream from the night before, the way I always do listen. It takes some listening because of his cleft palate but I listen all the same. Anyway I'm being smacked with that much spit that I have to look away. And I see over his shoulder that the seas are getting smaller. They're getting smaller. I look up to the cliffs and it really looks like the cliffs are receding. Can sort of feel the seas and cliffs being drawn back in and disappearing and becoming butterflies inside me. I have that feeling that today will be the start of my last day. (*He covers his eyes.*) I can see a picture of me running from your house. My heart's been ripped out and the ground underneath is loose underfoot. I'm running towards the harbour from this cliff. I can see the harbour being sucked into the sand and the cliffs pulled back like you would pull a curtain back. There's a great space now with me running over it towards nothing, towards...! No place. My heart's been ripped out, yet I can't stop running.

A pause. He lowers his hands from his eyes.

I can see all this... and then I'm back on the harbour with Simple Paddy and his cleft palate spitting over me.

A pause.

ADA. From this house you ran?

PATSY. Yes, Ada, from here.

BREDA. Leave, Patsy!

PATSY *leaves with* BREDA *slamming the door closed behind him.*

Why is it you allowed him to talk like that!?

ADA *marches over to a small table where an old tape recorder stands.*

ADA (*snaps*). Quiet!

ADA rewinds a tape.

CLARA. It's time, then.

CLARA stands and she and BREDA *watch* ADA's *every move.*

Won't you say who it is, Ada, please? Is it Breda the bad girl?

The tape stops. ADA *presses the play button and what begins is a foley soundtrack roughly pasted together by* ADA *to accompany the story we're about to hear.*

ADA. It's time and looking in the mirror and this feeling of everything not too right...

CLARA. Whose story, Ada?

ADA. It's time and looking in the mirror and this feeling...

CLARA. Ada?

ADA. ...of everything not too right, not too right. Up in the bathroom and my eighteen-year-old body...

CLARA. ...tries to shake off these...

ADA. Louder!

CLARA. ...tries to shake off these...

ADA. Louder, Clara!

CLARA. ...tries to shake off these doubts. Staring back behind the blusher and eyeshadow a girl who's yet to be kissed. Properly kissed.

ADA. Been mauled in the car park...

CLARA. Been mauled in the car park once outside The Sunshine Ballroom. Mauled by Jimbo 'The Face' Byrne, a fisherman stinking of stout and mackerel with the biggest face in the west. Crushed me up against his Ford Cortina and tore at my tits. Jimbo's head like an old horse all stooped and drunk. His fish fingers like hooks on my good blouse. But never been properly kissed...

ADA. But thoughts of him…

CLARA. Yes, thoughts of 'him' have me more forward thinking.

BREDA *starts to undress* CLARA *down to her slip.*

ADA. Louder.

CLARA. Thoughts of 'him' have me more forward thinking. For weren't they his words that asked me to meet him backstage? Wasn't it him that placed us together with that promise…

ADA. You meet me after.

CLARA. 'You meet me after.' And butterflies carry me down stairs. The soles of my feet tingling 'cause of 'him'. The top of my head all fizz! It's my time. It's my time.

ADA. You smell nice.

CLARA. Dad's voice stuck behind the newspaper and I tuck into my Saturday fry.

The rustling newspaper has me in mind of the crowd that'll gather tonight.

ADA. You meet me after.

CLARA. Packed so tight and faced towards the stage, we are. Clothes sparking off each other, shined leather shoes sticking on the dance floor. The chatter loud so you can't hear words and only these crackling noises. I polish off the bacon in double-quick time!

ADA *and* BREDA *grunt like pigs.*

ADA. Do it!

CLARA *grunts like a pig, joining* ADA *and* BREDA *in the grunting.*

BREDA *nonchalantly walks to the wall and takes down the 1950's rara skirt and the cashmere jumper.*

ADA *stops grunting.*

Sweet Breda.

CLARA. And through the door and Breda too made-up for the dance. Made-up in her nice blue skirt and red blouse... (*Suddenly forgets.*)

ADA. Her silent as usual! Mother slides...

CLARA. What?

ADA. Her silent as usual!

CLARA. Her silent as usual. Mother slides her fry towards her and like a little bird, her bites of the bacon. Like a little birdy! The rustling of the newspaper and her little lady bites. Her little lady bites. Her little lady bites! (*Mimics the birdlike noises and bites of* BREDA. *Snaps.*) 'Can't you eat like a humanfuckingbeing?!'

BREDA *starts dressing* CLARA *in the rara skirt and cashmere jumper.*

ADA. Time to leave...

CLARA. ...and each on our bike with the ten-mile cycle to The New Electric Ballroom spread out ahead like a yellow-brick road.

ADA. The town behind...

CLARA. ...and the cobblestone streets sewing it up all neat and perched by the sea, ahh look. We're away, Breda and me, with the... (*Again she's forgotten.*) With the...?

ADA. ...with the old road steering...

CLARA (*breaking down*). I can't...

ADA. ...with the old road steering us towards The New Electric.

CLARA. Breda, please...

ADA *grabs* CLARA *hard.* ADA *continues the story by herself.*

ADA. And move through the evening with pleated skirts hiding the busy legs beneath. They hide the things that want to be touched by him. They cover all desire and yet smouldering with each yard cycled. The breaths shorter, the freshly pressed blouses a little damp from the sweat. The make-up hot so that the face shimmers. So far behind The Sunshine Ballroom of our poxy harbour town and its lonely fishermen.

BREDA *applies make-up to* CLARA*'s face.*

Them fishermen mauling us like we're the fecking fish. Closing in on us, closing up the dance floor and backed into the corners 'til it's one on one. The lust in their faces. The heavy pants and sweaty palms. Their excuse for dancing? This rhythmless jumping up and down like they've just shit themselves. Which they have. Which they have! How they've trapped our little town in the Stone Age. Perched by the sea, this town needs drowning and reborn. (*Snaps.*) Clara!

CLARA. We cycle on, losing the memory of The Sunshine for The New Electric. The dusty road beneath turning to tarmacadam and the bigger town. The pace kicking us off our bicycles and how we now walk in this new town. Pushing out our little tits with a new confidence now. An American confidence!

ADA. That promise of…

CLARA. 'You meet me after.' His words have me queuing up outside The New Electric and pressed up against its wall.

ADA. Take a breath.

CLARA. For fear I'll blow up, a breath now, Clara.

A pause as CLARA *breathes and gathers herself.*

ADA. Slower.

CLARA (*slower now*). So leaned against the wall. Still have that little girl inside me.

I'm still sat on Mother's knee with hands all flour and cake. I'm still young enough to think of the world as family and town only. I'm at this moment. I'm at the edge of what it is to be a woman. I look from the corner and see all that I'm stepping into, like I'm moving from the black and white to the Technicolor. From nights mauled by fishermen to moments of wanted passion. Behind this wall… his words and desire and my new feelings of…

ADA (*faster now*). And enter then…

CLARA. And enter then…

ADA. And enter then…

CLARA. And enter…

Sounds of a dance floor and music played louder by ADA.

…and all is bodies. Bodies stuck together by numbers and sweat and music and beats and dance and cigarette smoke. And armless, legless bodies held up in a sea of skinny men in dark suits and young women's floral skirts. Already moving in a tide of badly suppressed sex… Oh, we move…

ADA. And Breda…

CLARA. …and Breda…? And Breda then separated, thank Christ. My last tie to home and the life before and Breda's ambition stuck… stuck in the cloakroom and soaked in mineral orange, the sap! Well, not me. Not Clara. Me, passed from stream to stream…

ADA. Louder!

CLARA. Me, passed from stream to stream and nearing the stage with lungs squeezed so tight. A mixture of torture and foreplay I can hear his voice crushing women's hearts and winning the admiration of any man with manhood but not quite the time to open my eyes to my man on stage. (*Slight pause.*) But open then… and there he is! 'The Roller Royle' and his showband. His stance… All-American. His suit a shade of blue right out of summer. His quiff, with no respect to gravity, whipped up on his head and reaching skywards. The Roller Royle. I hear his words from four weeks ago and my heart skips, my breath stops, my head races. 'You meet me after. You meet me after…'

BREDA. Done.

BREDA *is finished and* CLARA *has been fully transformed to her eighteen-year-old self.*

Well?

ADA (*nods*). Very good.

BREDA *sits and looks at the scene as it continues.*

CLARA. So afterwards then…

ADA. Wait, Clara!

ADA *then turns off the lights so that a single light isolates* CLARA *in the space.*

Afterwards…

CLARA. And backstage and pointed to where the Roller waits. Can hear his hit single, 'Wondrous Place', reel me in, his lovely voice soothing me and making this nervous scene a little easier. The corridor busy with people packing up and moving on to the next town but all thoughts are of him, Ada. Him and the things we will do together. Near his dressing room and my heart slower, my future mapped out with mornings met by his face and his sweet voice singing about this oh-so-wondrous place. The door a little open…

I enter.

A pause. Suddenly CLARA *gasps for air and her eyes fill with tears.*

He's sat on a table with you stood between his legs. (*Pause.*) He has his face tucked into you. (*Pause.*) His big hands around your tiny waist and he's kissing your mouth.

CLARA *looks to* BREDA.

My throat's jammed with those butterflies. My blood pumped slower. My heart shot all in an instant. It's your blue skirt and red blouse, Breda the bad girl. (*Slight pause.*) I can feel the hooked fingers of Jimbo 'The Face' Byrne tear at my blouse and rip out my heart and claim it

as his. I'm stood still… but I'm already running through
The New Electric, already travelling the ten miles home
and with each yard putting an end to any thoughts of love.
Each yard travelled and more distance between me and any
wish for what is… (*Almost spits.*) This love. The wind is
on my back, and the tide is inching in and the cobblestones
uneasy. The winding streets of our harbour town twisting
me to the inside. The narrow streets narrower somehow.
The houses on either side leaning in too close to me.
Telling me, squeezing me, hurrying me towards my inside.
Inside where's safe. Get inside, Clara. Get inside. Get
inside. Get inside. Get inside…

ADA *turns* CLARA *towards her and stares at her. ADA
turns the tape recorder off. She then goes and switches the
lights back on. She goes to the kitchen cupboard and opens
it. Inside, the cupboard is packed with the same type of
plain biscuits. She takes out one packet. She hands*
CLARA *a biscuit.*

I'm finished for now?

ADA *nods and then gently pats her on the head.*

Will I not have the nice coffee cake I made?

ADA *hands* BREDA *a biscuit.*

Will I not have some tea to wash down this biscuit, Ada?

A long pause. ADA *looks around the space and then at her
two sisters eating the plain biscuits. Suddenly, she fires the
packet of biscuits against the front door. Biscuits fly everywhere.*

The front door opens. It's PATSY *with another plastic tray
full of large fish.*

PATSY. All right, the ladies?

BREDA. Leave them where you stand and go.

PATSY *puts down the tray.* BREDA *goes about cleaning
up the biscuits.*

PATSY. Great to see Mary Calley fighting fit after her fall outside Bingo. I heard she had a few to drink and that would account for the terrible thump she gave the ground.

Popped her kneecap right open...

CLARA. That's enough, Patsy.

PATSY. She'll be using the walking stick for another month but that wouldn't put her out much. She only ever does two things as far as I can see, the pub and the Bingo and both of them involve sitting...

BREDA. Patsy!

PATSY. But you'd have to wonder the effects that concentration on a bingo sheet with a stomach full of Malibu has on your average seventy-year-old. That's the thing with age, you see. Medicine is well on top of its treatment to many people but the body of a pensioner is a bit of a lucky bag, isn't it? A routine treatment can uncover all manner of hidden diseases and random ailments. Phyllis Ryan went to the doctor's to get him to move his car and walked away with a burst appendix! I mean, that's a cruel lottery...

BREDA. Leave!

PATSY. Yes, Breda...

BREDA. Now, Patsy, that's enough!

PATSY. Out the door, out the door now, Breda!

PATSY looks towards the open door. Again, he looks very anxious. He can't leave.

Frustrated, he stamps on the ground hard.

SHITE!

The sisters don't react. PATSY then punches himself hard in the stomach. Again the sisters don't react. Again he punches his stomach hard. Again no reaction.

A very long pause.

PATSY. I saw Bernie Doyle in her front garden with all her grandchildren having a picnic and I've never seen such an amount of jelly in all my life. Mountains of it. (*Slight pause*.) I shouldn't have been there, I know that now. I shouldn't have. Sometimes my body has a will of its own and I find myself walking the little streets with no destination in mind. THESE BLOODY LEGS! (*Slight pause*.) I was across the road standing on the path and looking at the picnic and it was a lovely scene and her son, Bernie's son, he's a fisherman and his name is Finbarr, well, he's there with his lovely wife and his two kids and I shouldn't have done it, ladies, I know I shouldn't have done it, I shouldn't have done it!... but I started to imagine me as Finbarr. Me on his great big trawler out on the seas... though I wouldn't last a day on account of me getting seasick all the time... but I'm thinking about what it'd be like to have a meal with his lovely wife. What fish we'd order. I'm thinking in great detail then. Well, feck it, I stop all those thoughts 'cause it's cruel to me and to an outsider it's a bit creepy, so I give myself a good kick in the hole and I go to my dancing lessons in Sheila and Robert's house high on the hill, in their lovely sitting room with their paintings on the wall of exotic islands they've never visited. The waltzes and tangos and foxtrots and rumbas and we're learning the salsa at the moment and that's a great laugh, all right! Because there's only the three of us, and Sheila and Robert are a couple, I don't get to practise with another, so I'm just sitting there in their lovely sitting room and watching them dance and I start to think about Finbarr and his wife again. 'Stop it, Patsy, that's enough! STOP IT NOW!'(*Slight pause*.) And... And then suddenly I get this big hole in my stomach. The sort of hole you might fall into. And the more I look at Sheila and Robert and think of Finbarr and his wife, it feels like the walls of this hole are being scooped out by needles so that I'm doubled over in the armchair. And Robert's standing over me with my mouth all twisting from the pain of these needles, you see.... and feck it, I get up fast and leave and I'm walking the cobblestones and right above me are the seagulls gathering and they're sort of laughing at me 'cause I'm holding my stomach and doubled over. And it's tearing inside and with each second I get glimpses of me alone. Me in the bed... alone. Me on the streets... alone. Me staring at the cliffs receding... alone. At the beginning the seagulls are laughing. My walk quickens with the fucking seagulls following me and having a laugh. And then I hear one of them say, 'What is the purpose of you, Patsy? What is the purpose of you?' Well, I start to run now, 'cause that's a very hard question to answer and even harder when it's been asked by a bloody seagull! A seagull who's got the wings and the where-for-all to get the fuck out of town and fly off to somewhere else. What is the purpose of me? Too big a question. Run on, Patsy! And Mary Calley's looking from the pub with her busted leg put out on the table. And she sees me running past and her eyes all big then, her gob already wagging and spreading the gossip about 'Patsy the mad fishmonger', the bitch! Well, what 'as she got to gossip about when there's that amount of Malibu in her she's like her very own Caribbean island! Run on then! Run on! Run run run run! (*Pause.*) I stop and I'm standing at your door with these fish again. Look behind and see the cliffs receding. The seas being sucked back into the sand. The tides toing and froing all confused and restless... no sense to them. No sense to time. I'm back again at your door. (*Slight pause.*) Well, I start to think and try to get at least one thing clear. (*Pause.*) The only thing that is certain in my life is that I always come to this house. I come with the tide, don't I? And that is a certainty... and that certainty, it soothes me, somehow. It keeps the bigger question of 'purpose' at bay. It mightn't stop the seas shrinking or the cliffs receding but, that certainty, it does... soothe me.

A pause. The sisters remain quiet. Perhaps they're not even listening.

And before now I have never asked for anything. I have never asked why for all these years you've stayed inside, Clara and Breda. I don't ask that question for really I have no business asking. But if coming here is my only certainty and I have the same rhythm as these tides… I wonder now if you ladies would open up to me a little and treat me as a visitor some day. Have a good word to say to me even.

BREDA. Go.

PATSY. I won't return 'less I have a kind word.

BREDA. Don't be stupid, you'll return with the tide.

PATSY. But for what greater purpose?

BREDA. Leave.

PATSY. What purpose, Ada?!

ADA *walks over and holds the door for him.*

Ada?

Slight pause.

ADA. To bring the fish.

PATSY *leaves,* ADA *slamming the door closed behind him.*

CLARA *and* BREDA *go and place each tray of fish in a large chute in the wall as* ADA *stands, lost in her thoughts, looking at the front door.*

ADA *then opens the front door slowly and looks out.*

BREDA, *concerned, looks at* ADA. CLARA *stands looking at the cake.*

CLARA. She never did age, the Virgin Mary. You might put that down to the Middle-Eastern cuisine but Mary Magdalene had a face like a saddle and the truth is, a whore ages worse than someone clean.

BREDA. Clara!

CLARA (*sighs*). Will we ever eat this cake?

BREDA *increasingly concerned over* ADA*'s behaviour.*

24

ADA *remains looking out the front door at the outside as a beautiful golden light slowly fades up outside.*

ADA. I'm sitting in my office floating over the accounts changing fish into numbers.

Seconds and minutes are marking out time but it's the numbers that are marking me out. Making the rhythm of me, balancing me. I look up from the numbers and into the pattern of the day we've made here in this house. When I step out of the office I should be on my way home to your stories and the tea and the cake and Patsy and his fish... But I've stepped on to a beach and my very own new story now. And the sand's like cotton wool underfoot and when I look down the sand's golden. And the air all about me is warm, so it cannot be this island here. And no narrow streets and strange tides and talking seagulls... here the horizon open and light. There's a calm about me because the day has possibilities. And I'm calm because of that.

She covers her eyes with her hand.

But the sea is too still and there's no wind whatsoever and the clouds above are still. Nothing's moving because nothing's real. Like I'm standing in a picture of a beach and not the beach itself. A little child runs past. A six-year-old and I recognise her face when she turns around and smiles. I've seen her in old photographs and I know I'm looking at me running up this beach. She's the girl before you taught me these stories. (*Slight pause.*) I'm looking at her lying face down in a rock pool. I'm pulling her by the hair out of the water.

A pause. She lowers her hand from her eyes.

Things can never change here, can they?

CLARA *and* BREDA *remain silent.*

I really have to leave.

BREDA *walks intently towards the small table where the old tape recorder stands. She starts rewinding the tape.* ADA *turns and looks at her.*

CLARA (*rubbing her hands together, all excited*). It's time!
It's time!

ADA. Stop it, Breda!

The tape stops. CLARA *has gone to the door and slams it shut.*

BREDA *presses the play button and what begins is the same soundtrack by* ADA *to accompany the stories.*

BREDA. It's time and looking in the mirror and this feeling of everything not too right. Up in the bedroom and my seventeen-year-old body tries to shake off these doubts. Staring back behind the blusher and eyeshadow a girl who's already been kissed. Been properly kissed. Was it only four weeks ago in the car park outside The New Electric?

CLARA *starts undressing* BREDA *down to her slip.*

I was stood looking at the ground and every detail of that spot... the split tarmacadam, a plume of clover, its close proximity to the chip van... his hand in mine. The details. The Roller Royle. His hand on my waist and his words.

ADA *confused that it is* BREDA *leading the story.*

ADA. Breda, we don't...

BREDA. The details. The Roller Royle. His hand on my waist and his words...

ADA. Stop...

BREDA (*screams*). SAY IT!!

A slight pause.

ADA (*subdued*). 'We'll do it the next...'

BREDA. 'We'll do it the next time, Breda.' Little kiss then. Nothing too animal, more of a Gregory Peck. Turns away with his chips and my heart and into their van. Four weeks then. Four weeks 'til the next time, my first time.

CLARA *takes the 1950's blue pleated skirt and red blouse from the wall.*

ADA (*distant*). Mother calls…

BREDA. And down the stairs on butterflies and into the kitchen and Dad hidden behind the newspaper and the pig face of Clara at her bacon like a dog. The sad hateful face of my sister done up like a clown. How the other girls in the cannery laugh at her behind her stumpy back. Clara, dragging the family down with her mournful eyes and doughy skin. Take to my fry like a bird with my stomach churning with thoughts of the Roller Royle. Perfumed my bra and knickers in anticipation. Stood at the mirror that morning and slid my hands down my pants. Had a chit-chat conversation with myself as him, and took my hands to the rest of me. But tonight's the night. And each on our bike with the ten-mile cycle to The New Electric spread out ahead like a yellow-brick road. The town behind and the cobblestone streets sewing it up all neat and perched by the sea. Well, good enough for drowning and little else! Cycle on and on and feel like one of those Greek heroes taking to the seas, escaping into something better than the poxy Sunshine Ballroom with its oh-so-sad fishermen!

ADA. Buy you a mineral, Breda? Have a biscuit in the car park with me, Breda! (*Chants.*) Breda, Breda, Breda, Breda!

BREDA. And did once with Jimbo 'The Face' Byrne… a man with the biggest face in the west. Handed me his custard cream and asked me to lick the cream from the biscuit. Did so and saw him beating himself off, leaned against his Ford Cortina.

ADA. And enter then…

BREDA. And enter then…

ADA. And enter then…

BREDA. And enter…

Sounds of a dance floor and music played louder by ADA *as* CLARA *adds make-up to* BREDA*'s face.*

And all is bodies.

ADA. Louder!

BREDA. And all is bodies…

ADA. Bodies stuck together by numbers and sweat and music and beats and dance and cigarette smoke. And Clara then separated. My last tie to home shunted from my back and Clara's ambition stuck in the Hucklebuck with some sad someone else! But not Breda.

BREDA. Well, not me, lads. Not me. Me already steered towards the backstage. Steered as the Roller Royle serenades his Faithful. The women who'd gladly go all the way and the young men aping the great man himself.

ADA. Backstage…

BREDA. And the showband out front keeping time with my wanting heart. Into the Roller's dressing room and my skin is not my own. All alive it is! Tingling with images and giddy on love! Must settle for fear I blow up… and I do so… I do settle. Settle.

Settle. Settle, Breda. (*Slight pause.*) I start to think of me as a girl. Seventeen and I'm at the edge of things now. Leave behind the safety of all before…

ADA. Leave behind the safety of my home and our little town and step into the real world with love as my only guide.

BREDA *looks at* ADA.

With real love, Breda. Do you understand me?

BREDA *slaps* ADA *hard across the face.* ADA *shaken.*

BREDA *continues.*

BREDA. I can hear the band finishing up with 'Wondrous Place' and for a heartbeat… doubts raise their head. (*Slight pause.*) Door opens and there he is. Words are passed but to no point, no reason. The little room all charged with me and him… so no room for the words as he sits on a table and calls me over. I hold my head back, open my mouth a little and he kisses me softly. His fingers find their way down my back and slide into my pleated skirt and then round front 'til it stops on my belly. Tongues deeper and he lowers his hand then. Lowers it so it's in the perfumed knickers and I push into his hand. And I'm thinking I am his. He is mine certainly. His finger deeper and no doubts now. I can feel him through his pants and I know it's my time. I'm here at the start of a new life and it's my time. Door slams…

CLARA. …and someone there but gone.

BREDA. 'Stay put, I'll be back, I'll be back, Breda!' (*Quietly.*) Yes.

> CLARA *is finished changing* BREDA *into her seventeen-year-old self. She's squeezed into her blouse and skirt.*

> CLARA *then hands* BREDA *the show-business suit from the wall.*

> CLARA *turns off the lights but for the single light which isolates* BREDA.

> BREDA *is suddenly overcome and her eyes fill with tears.* ADA *instinctively takes advantage then.*

ADA (*snaps*). Breda! (*Prompting her.*) Outside then!

> BREDA *slowly shakes her head.*

BREDA (*quietly*). I can't.

> ADA *goes to her, grabs her by the shoulders and starts shaking her violently.*

ADA. Outside!

> ADA *stops.* BREDA *must continue until the end.*

BREDA. Outside and the moon lighting up the scene teasing me more. I can see him walking towards a new face standing in the same spot where I stood. That plume of clover just beneath her in the split tarmacadam. Her...? All Doris Day-like, all sweetness. He's moving in. I can see his big hand on her tiny waist. I can see him mouth the words... 'It's your time...' and little Doris folding into him now. (*Slowly.*) I'm standing, hugging his suit, Ada. My insides start retching. My mouth that he kissed all sour now, where he touched all muck. I'm still but already travelling the ten miles home and with each yard putting an end to any thoughts of love. Each yard travelled and more distance between me and any wish for what it is to be in love. And the wind is on my back and his song mocking me. And the narrow streets of our town they're narrower somehow. The houses on either side leaning in that bit close to me. They're squeezing me, hurrying me towards the inside of this house. To get inside. And stay inside always and keep safe away from this wondrous place. Keep safe. Keep safe inside always.

ADA *turns off the tape and* CLARA *switches back on the lights.*

A long pause. ADA *stares at* BREDA *who stands, alone and beaten.*

ADA. I'm only a baby when I first hear that story from you, Breda. Then thousands of times I've made you tell it again and again like some child... though I am not a child. (*Pause.*) Still, it hurts you just the same, isn't that right?

BREDA. Isn't this what we've tried to teach you? (*Slight pause.*) Don't you feel safer inside than out?

A slight pause.

ADA. I don't feel anything.

ADA *looks towards the front door.*

CLARA *stands looking at the cake again.*

CLARA. What would the Virgin Mary make of all of this, I wonder? Like many women I'd say she keeps an ordered house, but surely she'd have cause to worry for us three. I can almost feel my brain getting softer and it certainly feels like a nearer paradise.

Yes.

A slight pause.

(*Sighs.*) Will we ever eat this cake?

BREDA (*to* ADA). It's time for your rest and then we'll start over.

ADA *nods that she understands. She goes to a room and sits wide awake on the bed.*

BREDA *places the suit back on the wall. A long pause.*

CLARA. There's a lull. Sort of lull that can get you worried. Pass me the bowl, it's time!

BREDA *holds the bowl to her and* CLARA *puts her hand into it. She's very excited. She picks out the one folded up piece of paper that's in there. She unwraps it and reads.*

(*Surprised.*) 'No man is an island'!

BREDA *turns over an hourglass.*

BREDA. Begin.

BREDA *begins to take off her 'costume'.*

CLARA. By their nature people are talkers. You can't deny that. You could but you'd be affirming what you're trying to argue against and what would the point of that be? No point. Just adding to the sea of words that already exist out there in your effort to say that people are not talkers. But people talk and no one in their right mind would challenge that. Unless you're one of those poor souls starved of vocal cords or that Willy Prendergast boy who used live in town and only managed three words. One was 'yes', one was 'no' and one was 'fish'. But even he talked. People are born talkers. Those present when a baby comes into the world are made all too aware that the womb is a more desirable place for a baby. That and the unglamorous entrance the baby must make. For all his miracles and great creations, you'd imagine our Lord could have created a more dignified point of arrival. This is the man who did wonders with the mouth and ears and surpassed Himself with the eyes but sharing a channel with the 'waterworks department' doesn't strike me as the healthiest environment for a yet-to-be-born baby. And I'm not even a plumber. But people get set in their ways early on. Spat out into the world with this feeling of superiority, some people! Stuck in the pram and already the prime spot! Sat opposite me and already the pristine doll...

BREDA. Stuck in the pram, the lumpen pig. Sat opposite me, Mother's little gargoyle...

CLARA. I'm standing looking at your underwear laid out on the bed. I can smell the perfume and it's you who sends me off to the bathroom with a stomach full of doubts!

BREDA. On with the underwear and already you sitting there on my back. Stuck there with your face the picture of this town. The happy pig at the trough with your thoughts of The Sunshine Ballroom. Taking the biscuit in the car park, hey, Clara?! Opening your zip for Jimbo 'The Face'. (*Chants.*) Clara, Clara, Clara, Clara!

CLARA. And cycling the ten miles to The New Electric and you as always po-faced. Like a big plank there! A long streak of misery. Off the bike with tits out and how they look at you, these boys... such indifference.

BREDA. Off the bike and sweat clinging to your hairy back. You smelling like a damp April day though everywhere else is summer. Stood in the queue and again I've got you staining my style. You with your slap-happy face and doughy body stood outside The New Electric like a dressed-up Neanderthal...

CLARA. And enter then...

BREDA. And enter then...

CLARA. And enter then…

BREDA. And enter and get busy throwing you off my back…

CLARA. Throwing you off my back!

BREDA. And 'Wondrous Place' and seconds away from your big heartache.

CLARA. You and the Roller. The big romantic scene…

BREDA. And his hand on my back, and his hand down my front, and his mouth against my mouth. While you're stood there with that face collapsing into tears…

CLARA. And you stood outside in the car park with your sodden perfumed knickers, your stony face for once cracking into some emotion as the Roller rolls on to Doris Day…

BREDA. Bitch!

CLARA. Gobshite!

BREDA. Shut it!

CLARA. A cup of tea a cup of tea a cup of tea!

BREDA. We can't have tea!

CLARA. Where's me tea!?

BREDA. She won't give us any tea.

CLARA. ME CAKE, ME CAKE!!

BREDA (*covering her ears*). We can't have the cake!

CLARA. Me on her lap and I mix the flour with the eggs and the sugar and the coffee…

BREDA. I MADE THE BLOODY CAKE!!

CLARA. And I'm half-listening to the radio and her leg sends me up and down like I'm on a horse trotting.

BREDA *walks fast towards the coffee cake.*

Not galloping now! Never a gallop. She never does anything to harm me, what with me being her favourite! I want my cake, I want my cake...

BREDA *picks up the coffee cake and violently flings it towards* CLARA. *It smashes and disintegrates on the floor.*

A pause as they both look down on it.

CLARA *lets out a scream of complete anguish.*

Enter PATSY *fast with more fish.*

PATSY. All right, the ladies?

CLARA (*screams*). GET OUT!

In an act of defiance PATSY *throws the tray of fish on the ground.*

PATSY. Despite my best efforts to stay away I'm back with this tide. No rhyme, no reason, no purpose. As always the bleak welcome...

He goes to leave.

BREDA. Stay.

PATSY *turns back.*

Close the door.

PATSY. You want me to step inside? Like a visitor?

BREDA. Do it.

PATSY *closes the door.*

A long pause. PATSY *can hardly believe he's finally inside.*

CLARA, *sobbing over the cake, mumbles a 'Hail Mary' to herself.*

Speak to me about your romantic loves.

PATSY. There's nothing to speak of. It's not that I hadn't wished it but in a town this size we've all got our roles to play and mine is to play a man of no great purpose... Might I sit down...

BREDA. Don't be getting ahead of yourself!

PATSY. Yes, Breda.

A slight pause as BREDA *stares at a very self-conscious* PATSY.

BREDA. Off with your clothes.

A slight pause.

PATSY. My clothes?

BREDA. Isn't it like me you are?! Now off with your clothes, Patsy.

PATSY. I don't feel that way about you, Breda....

BREDA. Do it! Clara... Water!

PATSY (*to himself*). Jesus.

PATSY *nervously starts taking off his clothes.* CLARA *fills a basin of water.*

BREDA. What chance the baby, Patsy? Only born and spat out into dirt. Little baby lying in the cot listening to the words clogging the air. Stepping outside and finding his feet and the poor baby marked by even more words. What chance to keep him clean when the poor creature's turned grubby from the amount of words filling the space, filling your head. Stamped by story, aren't we, Patsy?! So what chance any man or woman against the idle word? The idle word?! Sure, there's no such thing as the idle word. Branded, marked and scarred by talk. Boxed by words, Patsy. Those bitches in the cannery and the gossip rising above the machines. All talk of Clara and Breda and The New Electric and the Roller Royle and the broken hearts. Mocking talk all week turning the streets narrower around us. Them nasty words crashing about from Monday to Friday and locking that front door behind us. What chance for the broken-hearted and the fishmonger to keep clean when people have the making of us? No mystery, no surprise...

CLARA. ...no chance.

BREDA. Marked from early on. What words do you hear branding you, Patsy? 'Lonesome', surely? And 'lumpen' and 'ugly' and 'lonely' and 'foolish' and 'fishy', surely. Surely 'fishy'. Here he is, the 'fishy' fishmonger. And how you might pass and hear all those other words, at once, chasing you, Patsy. Chasing you through the little streets. Well, no more, hey! Isn't it time for a rewrite?

PATSY (*excited*). It's well time, Breda! Well time!

PATSY *stands in his shabby underpants in the basin of water with* CLARA *ready to scrub him clean.*

BREDA. Scrub away then and reborn, Clara!

CLARA *starts vigorously scrubbing him.*

Off with them words and all those stories pasted together and stuck on your back. Wipe away all them lazy images that others pin on us, Patsy. Get clean of that awful smell of fish and guts while you're at it. Strip away letter by letter and them terrible words will surely fall, won't they?! Fall back to the rot where they belong.

CLARA (*struggling with the smell*). Christ!

BREDA. Right out of the hospital and the little baby boy all powdered fresh and standing right here in front us, by Christ! Cleaner than clean with not a single word in earshot against him. No words to name and brand. Like you were spat out of your mother and found yourself standing in your underpants right here in our front room all these years later.

CLARA *continues for a while and then stops scrubbing him.*

CLARA (*catching her breath*). He's done.

PATSY (*smells his skin*). Jesus, like baby skin.

BREDA. And start then.

BREDA *hands the Roller Royle's suit to* CLARA *who starts to dress* PATSY *in it.*

…With the good news spread like wildfire. Standing out into town and the world is claimed as his in an instant. Caught unawares and the world's taken by 'the one and only' as he walks about town and everything moves to his pulse. The cars being pumped along the cobblestones, the little to and fro of people popping in and out of their houses, the shifting patterns of light on the water, even the tides themselves… everything moving for him, from him. The whole world his Faithful. The women who'd gladly go all the way and the young men aping the great man himself.

PATSY. Such pants.

BREDA. Sure, what woman could remain upright with this man about? Some heartless, bloodless, idiot dyke but no other woman, surely? And people's great weapon of words at first seduced and silenced, overawed and struck dumb. At first this silence, but then slowly from a whisper it grows. Oh, it grows, Clara, can't you hear it?

CLARA. Oh, I can, Breda, I can!

BREDA. It starts in a quiet breath and takes to the air, Patsy. A little breeze gets a hold of it and moves it about the house and towards the door and outside. Outside then and a breeze along the cobblestones takes it and through the little sewn-up streets it moves. It moves from breath to breath and the breeze stronger and it stronger too and it's taken to the harbour where the bigger wind takes a hold of it. And passed from breath to breath over the bay and sea and shared out amongst the airstreams it takes to the world and is taken in every breath in every word to everyone. Do you know what it is?

PATSY. Not a clue, Breda.

BREDA. 'Adoration.' Adoration for one man.

CLARA. That suit looks lovely on ya, Patsy.

The new PATSY *transformed in the Roller's suit.*

PATSY (*overawed*). Jesus, Mary and Joseph.

BREDA. Sit down at the table and a new day for us then.

PATSY *sits.*

ADA *walks out from her bedroom and sees* PATSY *sitting at the table. She stops. He immediately stands.*

I thought it time for a visitor.

A pause. PATSY *feeling very self-conscious as* ADA *just stares at him in the suit. She then goes to the table and sits opposite him.*

BREDA *puts a plate of two plain biscuits in front of them. He's a little taken aback with the pathetic lunch but* PATSY *begins to eat it nevertheless.* ADA *picks up her biscuit and starts to eat it too.*

A very long pause.

PATSY. No chance of a cup of tea? It's a little dry.

There's no answer. He continues to eat the biscuit.

ADA. What is it you have to say to me, Patsy? Something new maybe?

PATSY. Something… new? (*Slight pause.*) Yes.

Deep breath and nervously PATSY *stands up and settles himself. He then speaks.*

The, emmm… the little cobblestones…

BREDA. Louder, Patsy.

He resumes.

PATSY. The… little cobblestones and they take me to the harbour. I meet you by the harbour, Ada. You're there in your good clothes and me in this terrific suit. And we talk about the fish in the seas and whether the fish have any notion of what awaits them on the land. Christ, if they only knew the torture that awaited them, surely they wouldn't be swimming in packs…

CLARA. New, Patsy! New!

PATSY. So, ahhhh… So, anyway… we're walking through the town and up through the little streets and we can hear the gossip from inside the houses, so you hold my hand then…

BREDA (*prompting him*). And your beautiful face.

PATSY. What?

BREDA. Say it!

PATSY (*fast*). …and then Bernie Doyle, she's there… and we're having a conversation about Nana Cotter's one-hundredth birthday party and the great selection of sandwiches that were on display…

BREDA. And your beautiful face!

PATSY. And Mr Simmons limps over and we're talking about his new hip.

Apparently it doesn't need any lubrication which is news to me as I was always under the impression…

BREDA. Patsy!

CLARA (*covers her ears and barks*). Fish yes yes. No yes fish.

PATSY (*panicking*). …We're walking up the hill now, Ada, and the climb of the hill is lesser to us. Past the cannery and into Sheila and Robert's house and Robert's putting on his dancing-instruction video and going through the moves with real precision and dedication, fair play to him…

ADA *stands and turns away from him.*

…and I'm no longer sitting in the corner just watching but I'm centre stage with the lovely you now, Ada. Me and the lovely Ada and we're dancing with the pictures of all these exotic islands around us and Robert sipping on a soda water and saying what a great match me and Ada are. 'You're a great match, you two!'… He says…

ADA *goes towards the front door.*

…And afterwards and we're all having a game of Scrabble which I win with the word 'haddock'… a triple-word winner…

ADA *opens the door and* PATSY *thankfully stops talking.*

A long pause as ADA *looks out on the outside and the three others look at her.*

CLARA. There's a lull. Sort of lull that can get you worried. Pass me the bowl, Breda, it's time!

ADA. You can leave now, Patsy.

PATSY. Romance doesn't come too easy for a fishmonger, Ada. You can see I tried…

ADA. You leave, I stay, that's the order of things here.

PATSY. But maybe a song…

BREDA. Leave, she said.

PATSY. Music can say it better than these awful words, surely!

PATSY *frantically putting a cassette into the tape recorder.*

BREDA. Go, Patsy! Away from the door, Ada!

PATSY. Just one more chance! Fuck it, one more go! Something to fan the flames of love! The music's playing, so the lights to set the scene, Ada, please! Please! Please!

PATSY *stands on the table, ready to sing his song.*

The opening chords to 'Wondrous Place' begins.

The door remains open. ADA *turns off the light inside.* PATSY *lit only by the light streaming through the open door.*

PATSY *sings for* ADA. *He begins nervously.*

> I found a place full of charms,
> A magic world in my baby's arms.
> Her soft embrace like satin and lace –
> Wondrous place.

What a spot in a storm,
To cuddle up and stay nice and warm.
Away from harm in my baby's arms –
Wondrous placc.

Man, I'm nowhere
When I'm anywhere else,
But I don't care,
Everything's right when she holds me tight.

Her tender hands on my face,
I'm in heaven in her embrace.
I wanna stay and never go away –
Wondrous place.

Instrumental.

Man, I'm nowhere
When I'm anywhere else,
But I don't care,
Everything's right when she holds me tight.

Her tender hands on my face,
I'm in heaven in her embrace.
I wanna stay and never go away –
Wondrous place.

PATSY *performs wonderfully. It finishes with the air charged with something new.* BREDA *switches the light back on.* PATSY *a little self-conscious.*

A song my poor dead mother taught me.

BREDA (*very hesitant*). Was she pretty, your mother?

PATSY (*staring at* ADA). Like Doris Day, they said. And him a decent singer, though I never learnt of his name or met him even. Last thing I had to do with him was my conception in the car park…

ADA. Of The New Electric Ballroom.

A slight pause.

PATSY. Yeah.

BREDA *remains standing and slowly pisses herself. A small pool forms around her feet.* ADA *looks at this happening and then back to* PATSY.

ADA. Doesn't story always find a way to catch us out, Patsy?

PATSY (*innocently*). It does. Story's a funny fish, all right.

A pause.

ADA (*a little confused*). What a difference you are to me suddenly. (*Pause.*) Time to start anew, you and me?

PATSY. Yes please, Ada.

ADA *stares directly into* PATSY'*s eyes. A pause.*

ADA (*softly*). The town still asleep I cycle to the cannery as always. I sit in my office with the machines crashing inside and tinning the fish. I look over my accounts and turn fish into numbers. I cycle home and the town quiet as always. I see people but talk to no one. A day like any other day. (*Pause. Somewhat nervous.*) But a different day… because of you. Everything coloured by you, every movement, each second passed is touched by you. The town sewn up by you. Tone and air changed knowing that you are close to me. It's me and you, you and me. (*Pause.*) And then it starts as a quiet whisper 'tween two little old ladies who watch us pass by. And it takes to the air. A little breeze gets a hold of it and moves it along the cobblestones and through the sewn-up streets it moves. It moves from breath to breath and the breeze stronger and it stronger too and it's taken to the harbour where the bigger wind takes a hold of it. And passed from breath to breath over the bay and sea and shared out amongst the airstreams it takes to the world and is taken in every breath in every word to everyone. (*Pause.*) The world knows of our new love. It's love.

PATSY. It's love. (*Pause.*) I'm standing in the little shoebox I call my bedroom, Ada.

I'm standing in my underpants and I'm staring down on my little bed. The pillows dented from where we lay our heads. The shape of us marked out on the bed, mapping out our night's sleep. The house quiet as always. The little stairs groaning as always. Everything as always but for this warm feeling in my belly. You're sat in the kitchen waiting there, Ada. And you touch my face. We're at the edge of things now and about to leave behind the safety of all we've known before. So turn to the door and open a life of possibility...

ADA. And enter then...

PATSY. And enter then...

ADA. And enter then...

PATSY. And enter then...

ADA. And enter then...

PATSY. And enter the outside and the cobblestones and sewn-up streets and salty air and the possibility for further away. The outside and destinations unknown and my world blown right open by 'chance', by this chance to change. And in an instant I'm part of the living, the free, the 'fateless', the unmarked and I can see me joining those seagulls and taking my pick of life, and led by airstream and breeze, my life made open by your hand in mine. Your hand is in mine and showing me the open road of possibility, a horizon of chance and what then? Like being taken to the harbour and just a little drop we are. And taken by the tides and out further by waves and currents and further and further still until our little town is a sad memory, a bad joke.

My life a sudden adventure with my hand in yours. So what details then? What details, Patsy!? Suddenly I'm drunk on possibility! We're sheltering from the rain and you kiss me. I'm curled against your back listening to your snores. I'm sat on the bed and smiling at you singing in the bath. I'm holding you in my arms with you twitching between sleep and wake. I'm watching you laugh at something stupid I said. We're stood in a crowd and you're touching my back. We're dancing in Sheila and Robert's with our faces together. We're sitting in Bingo and filling in the same sheet. We're stood at the harbour and watching the horizon and we take to the sea then and the waves take us and the world opens to us further and further and I'm holding your hand. Your hand holding my hope. Your hand holding my hope. Your hand. (*Pause.*) Christ! Already something's got a hold of me. In one breath all love is good and it keeps me and this love it fills me... but with each step taken and a different love, a fragile love, a love blind, surely. I let go of your hand and walk away fast. And I want for the lover's walk and the lie-ins and the kisses and the sweet remembered details, the slow romance and the sudden lust of love, but my heart tells me that the risk is far too great. It's too great, Ada! We're walking hand in hand but you're not really there. We're sitting side by side but you are somewhere else maybe. I'm curled against your back but your back's colder to me somehow. I'm kissing you with a kiss that lasts seconds too less for me but seconds too more for you. It's not you, it's not you! And what words do you pin to me? 'Lonesome', surely. And 'lumpen' and 'ugly' and 'lonely' and 'fishy', surely. Surely 'fishy'. A man whose only companion is fish and now sewn together with another heart?! Fuck it! My own heart's too scarred by days and nights alone. Too set in its ways by years of chit-chat to little old ladies. Too scared to face into the unknown with just love as a map! I'm stood still but already travelling the lonely road and with each yard travelled it's more distance between me and any wish for what it is to be in love, this reckless love! And the wind is on my back and the seagulls above mocking me! The narrow streets of our town they're narrower. The houses on either side leaning in that bit close. They're squeezing me, hurrying me away from any possibility of a different life! My heart's ripped out and the ground underneath is loose with the cliffs receding. I see the harbour being sucked into the sand and the cliffs pull back like you would pull a curtain back. And now this great space with me running over it towards nothing, towards no home, towards no place, Patsy. My heart ripped out and I can't stop running! I can't stop!

A long pause. ADA, *frozen in shock, is looking towards* PATSY *for some explanation for what she's just heard.* PATSY *can't look at her.* BREDA *and* CLARA *look at* ADA *and await her response. Suddenly* ADA *gasps for air. For the very first time her eyes have filled with tears.* PATSY *turns and leaves fast for the outside. The front door slams shut by itself behind him.*

BREDA *presses the tape recorder and a new story is told.*

BREDA. It's time and looking in the mirror and this feeling of everything not too right.

Stood in the bedroom and your forty-year-old body tries to shake off these doubts.

Staring back a woman who's never been kissed.

CLARA. And it was only yesterday…

BREDA. And it was only yesterday and happy with the pattern of things. When routine woke you with the familiar… the pattern safe, life given a purpose. And what now all of a sudden…?

CLARA *begins to dress* ADA *in the rara skirt and red blouse.*

'Cause still staring back, a woman who's never been kissed. So outside and take to the streets and cycle to the cannery and the machines, to those distant voices and bad words that locked the door. And inside, inside then. And the stories take over and our pattern returns.

CLARA. The lovely pattern of things.

BREDA. By their nature people are talkers. You can't deny that. You could but you'd be affirming what you're trying to argue against and what would the point of that be?

BREDA *aggressively swipes* ADA's *face with lipstick.*

Just adding to the sea of words that already exist out there in your effort to say that people are not talkers. But people talk.

CLARA. Fish fish fish. Yes no fish! No yes fish!

A very long time where BREDA, CLARA *and* ADA *are silent.*

ADA, *costumed ridiculously, face covered in lipstick, stands with tears streaming down her face.* CLARA *sits and stares down on the remains of the sponge cake.*

BREDA *stands still and silent, holding and listening to the tape recorder as the sounds continue for a while. She turns it off.*

Then.

Will we have a cup of tea and some of that nice cake you made, Breda?

BREDA. Yes, Clara.

A pause.

ADA. Will I make the tea, Breda?

BREDA. That would be nice.

ADA *goes to the kettle and turns it on and watches it boil.*

It boils.

Blackout.

Silence.

The End.

The New Electric Ballroom premiered at the Kammerspiel Theatre in Munich, Germany, on September 30, 2004, under the direction of Stephan Kimmig. It received its English-language premiere by The Druid Theatre in Galway, Ireland, on July 14, 2008, with Rosaleen Linehan as Breda, Val Lilley as Clara, Catherine Walsh as Ada and Mikel Murfi as Patsy. It was directed by Enda Walsh, designed by Sabine Dargent, with lighting by Sinéad McKenna and sound by Gregory Clarke.

On August 3, 2008, the same production opened at the Traverse Theatre in Edinburgh, Scotland, as part of the 2008 Edinburgh Festival Fringe. The production was revived for an international tour, with Ruth McCabe taking over the role of Clara. It was performed throughout Ireland beginning on April 7, 2009. It began a run at the Perth International Arts Festival in Australia beginning on February 17, at Riverside Studios in London starting on March 3, then at St. Ann's Warehouse in Brooklyn, New York, beginning on October 27.

THE WALWORTH FARCE

"An unsettling but exhilarating blend of the hilarious with the horrifying."

"Walsh has outdone himself with a new play more complex, dark and emotionally rich than any of his previous efforts . . . it rewards with a theatrical experience that claws at the imagination for days afterwards."

"It is exhilarating to hang on for dear life on a ride through Mr. Walsh's bold, original imagination. *The Walworth Farce* is as brilliant an original as you are likely to see in the theatre this year."

B oth brilliant and savage, this is a tale of an Irish father and his two sons stuck for nineteen years in a decaying London flat, daily replaying a tale of the father's own invention. *The Walworth Farce* is about what can happen when we become trapped in the stories we tell about our lives.

The Walworth Farce, a companion piece to *The New Electric Ballroom*, was first produced by The Druid Theatre in Galway. In 2007, it won the Edinburgh Fringe First Award and received its U.S. premiere at St. Ann's Warehouse in 2008 in Brooklyn.

ENDA WALSH is a Dublin born playwright who now lives in London. His plays have been translated into twenty languages. Among his best known plays are *Disco Pigs* and *Bedbound*. He has received two Edinburgh Fringe First awards in consecutive years for *The Walworth Farce* and *The New Electric Ballroom*. He wrote the screenplay for *Hunger* (2008), the story of the final days of IRA hunger striker Bobby Sands, which won numerous awards, including the Camera d'Or at the Cannes Film Festival.

THE WALWORTH FARCE

THE WALWORTH FARCE

Enda Walsh

THEATRE COMMUNICATIONS GROUP
NEW YORK
2009

The Walworth Farce and *The New Electric Ballroom* is published by Theatre Communications Group, Inc., 520 Eighth Avenue, 24th Floor, New York, NY 10018-4156, by special arrangement with Nick Hern Books Limited.

The Walworth Farce and *The New Electric Ballroom* were first published in Great Britain by Nick Hern Books Limited in association with the Druid Theatre Company.

A CIP catalog record for this book is available from the Library of Congress.

ISBN-13: 978-1-55936-354-9

Cover photos: George Marks, Hulton Archive/Getty Images (Ballroom); Three Lions, Hulton Archive/Getty Images (Walworth).

Cover design by John Gall

First TCG Edition, October 2009

To the first director of this play
Mikel Murfi
for his advice, support, enthusiasm and general brilliance.
Thank you so much.

Characters

in order of appearance

DINNY, *fifty, Irish accent*
BLAKE, *twenty-five, Irish accent*
SEAN, *twenty-four, Irish accent*
HAYLEY, *twenty-four, South London accent*

This text went to press before the end of rehearsals and may differ slightly from the play as performed.

ACT ONE

The set is three square spaces. Essentially a living room at its centre, a kitchen to stage left and a bedroom to stage right.

Much of the plasterboard has been removed from the walls and what remains are the wooden frames beneath.

The two doors on the wall leading into the kitchen and the two doors leading into the bedroom on the other wall have been removed.

The back wall shows the front door leading into this flat.

There are two wardrobes at the back made from the plasterboard. One on the left and one on the right of the front door.

The decor is at best drab. Everything worn and colourless and stuck in the 1970s.

There is an armchair and a small coffee table in the sitting room with six cans of Harp on it. The kitchen is fitted and very messy. The bedroom has two single beds on top of each other made to look like bunk beds.

We're in a council flat on the Walworth Road, South London.

As the lights go up we see a man sitting in the armchair. This is the father, DINNY. He wears a bad brown yellowing wig on his head, a tight ill-fitting suit that makes him look clownish. He has a jet black bushy moustache. He's holding a small biscuit tin.

On a side table next to him he presses the button of an old tape recorder. 'An Irish Lullaby' begins to play. Slowly he opens the biscuit tin. He looks inside, smiles and smells the contents. He closes it and places it under the armchair. He begins to polish his shoes with a tin of brown polish.

His son BLAKE stands in his vest and underpants and irons something on a coffin-shaped cardboard box in the bedroom.

5

BLAKE's brother SEAN *stands in the kitchen. He wears a woollen hat. He takes it off and places it in the pocket of his jacket. His hair has been shaved so that he looks as if he's badly balding.*

He goes to the table where he looks into a Tesco bag. His expression suddenly shocked. He takes out an extremely large salami sausage. He goes to the oven and flings the sausage inside, closing the door. With trepidation he returns to the Tesco bag, reaches in and takes out a packet of Ryvita crackers. Again he's shook.

DINNY *enters the kitchen carrying the tape recorder and* SEAN *quickly hides the Ryvita behind his back.* DINNY *pours himself a glass of water and gargles for a bit.* SEAN *watches him.* DINNY *spits it back in the sink, turns and exits the kitchen and back into the sitting room.*

DINNY *places the tape recorder on the side table and starts to do little physical jerks. He's exercising.*

BLAKE *is putting on what he was ironing. A floral skirt. He puts the iron under the bed and takes up a freshly ironed colourful blouse. He smells it. It's not the best. He sprays it with some Mister Sheen. He smells it again and puts it on. From under the bed he takes an old lamp with an orange floral shade. He slings it off a hook that hangs from the ceiling and turns it on. The bedroom is thrown into a new light.*

SEAN *meanwhile is making Ryvita sandwiches in the kitchen with spreadable cheese he's taken from a tiny fridge.*

DINNY *stops exercising. He takes off his wig and we can see some Velcro tape running on top of his head which obviously keeps on the wig. He takes a comb out and gives the wig a quick once over.*

BLAKE *puts on a woman's black permed wig. He picks up the cardboard coffin and exits the bedroom and into the sitting room and stands waiting.*

SEAN *sticks a bad fake moustache on (à la Magnum P.I.), dons a tight cream sports jacket which he buttons up and exits the kitchen.* BLAKE *hands him the coffin and enters one of the wardrobes.*

SEAN *stands holding the coffin on his shoulders by the front door and waits for his father.*

DINNY *sticks his wig back on. He goes to the wall and takes a small golden trophy off a shelf. He reverentially kisses it before carefully replacing it. He blesses himself.*

He takes a deep breath and exhales sharply. He's ready.

DINNY *holds the other end of the coffin with* SEAN. *He reaches to the light switch on the back wall and switches off the light in the sitting room as 'An Irish Lullaby' comes to an end.*

The room is thrown into darkness and silence. DINNY *immediately turns the light back on.*

DINNY. She was our mother, Paddy –

> *Suddenly the tape recorder blasts out the Irish traditional song 'A Nation Once Again'.*

> *The two of them startled.*

Shite!

DINNY *turns off the tape recorder. Again he takes a deep breath and exhales sharply. He then reaches back to the light switch and turns the lights off again. He immediately turns them back on.*

> *The Farce begins. The three speak in Cork City accents. The performance style resembles The Three Stooges.*

She was our mother, Paddy, and she treated us well.

SEAN AS PADDY. It was a happy outcome, Dinny, even if it was her funeral.

DINNY. To see her little smiling face all done up in that make-up, looking like a movie star, wasn't she?

SEAN AS PADDY. A little miracle how her head was recreated when you think of the wallop that horse gave her. Hit by a dead horse. Who would have believed it?

DINNY. As the priest said, Paddy . . . only the good Lord knows of our final curtain.

SEAN AS PADDY. I fear He does.

DINNY. It was God's will to send a massive dead stallion careering over a hedge.

SEAN AS PADDY. Yes.

DINNY. God's will to send it crashing on top our sweet mother's tiny body as she innocently picked gooseberries for her own consumption on that quiet country road. Whatever way you look at it, Paddy, religion's awful cruel.

SEAN AS PADDY. Is that cans of beer over there?

DINNY. It is, they are.

SEAN AS PADDY. It's just she's getting awful heavy . . .

DINNY. Stick her in the dining room there, Paddy. Don't want my two little boys having nightmares.

SEAN *and* DINNY *take the coffin into the bedroom.*

SEAN AS PADDY. So this is your place, Dinny?

DINNY. Built with my own hands . . . figuratively speaking of course. Not much call for building work in my line of work.

BLAKE AS MAUREEN *enters from the wardrobe.*

BLAKE AS MAUREEN. You want me to fix the sandwiches, Dinny?

DINNY. Go heavy on the cheese spread, sweetheart. You know how I like my sandwiches, Maureen love.

BLAKE AS MAUREEN. Where's the kitchen?

DINNY *secretly and aggressively points over to where it is.*

BLAKE AS MAUREEN *quickly enters the kitchen. He immediately takes off his wig and puts on a new red-haired permed wig and re-enters the wardrobe.*

SEAN AS PADDY. What is it you do again, Dinny?

DINNY. Brain surgery, Paddy.

SEAN AS PADDY. And to think you were thrown out of school at fifteen.

DINNY. Ireland's a terrible hole and you'll get no argument from me . . . but I'll say this about it . . . it gives fools a fighting chance.

SEAN AS PADDY. Fair play.

DINNY. Not like London, Paddy?

SEAN AS PADDY. London's a tough old nut. For a while I was working the sites but London's all grown up now and not much building for fellas like me. Truth is I haven't worked for six years, Dinny.

DINNY. You've flat feet of course.

SEAN AS PADDY. The flat feet are only half of it, there's more. Being a man of medicine you may have heard of my condition.

DINNY. You've got a condition?

SEAN AS PADDY. A critical condition.

DINNY. Proceed.

SEAN AS PADDY. I'm getting pains in my hole, Dinny.

DINNY (*carefully*). Yes.

SEAN AS PADDY. Remember as a little boy that big railing I impaled myself on . . . pierced my back?

DINNY. Oh that hole!

SEAN AS PADDY. It just missed the heart, didn't it. When I get too excited, Dinny, I fall over . . .

DINNY. Do ya?

SEAN AS PADDY. I do! Blood stops racing to the head . . . I collapse.

DINNY. Collapse!? Good Lord!

SEAN AS PADDY. Doctor says one day I might never wake up. Thought it might happen to me today what with Mammy and everything.

DINNY. You had a pain in your hole today?

SEAN AS PADDY. A shocking pain in my hole, Dinny.

DINNY. Well, you listen to me, little brother. I wasn't always there for you in the past.

SEAN AS PADDY. You were never there for me.

DINNY. That's right, you're right. But in the future. If there's anything you want, if that hole of yours is keeping you awake at night just pick up the telephone and give us a call.

Enter BLAKE AS VERA *from the wardrobe.*

BLAKE AS VERA. Those two boys of yours are terrorising a copper outside.

DINNY. The little feckers. Sort that out for us, Paddy.

SEAN AS PADDY *runs and disappears into the wardrobe closing the door behind him.*

BLAKE AS VERA. Well, haven't you done well for yourself!? Beautiful leather couch, lovely little ornaments. Nice shag carpet. That seen any action has it?

DINNY. Now a gentleman wouldn't say, Vera.

BLAKE AS VERA. He wouldn't but you would.

DINNY *and* BLAKE AS VERA *laugh.*

DINNY (*laughing*). Oh very good, very good!

BLAKE AS VERA. How'd you make the big leap from painting and decorating to brain surgery?

DINNY. Oh you might well ask that question, Vera love.

BLAKE AS VERA. I just did, Denis.

A pause.

DINNY. One day . . .

BLAKE AS VERA. Yes?

DINNY *really has to think hard about this.*

DINNY. . . . a few years ago . . . I was busy applying some paint to a client's wall. Now she was a woman who was forever complaining about headaches and such like.

'Denis,' she would say, 'I have such a terrible pounding in the head.' Well, the poor dear fell in front of me and cracked her head wide open. And there I was looking at my first brain. (*Easier now.*) Now I liken the brain to a walnut, Vera. Larger obviously and not the class of thing you'd hand out to kiddies at Hallowe'en . . . but a walnut all the same. She was still breathing so I had to act fast. Now Coca-Cola, which I had on my person for its thirst-quenching properties, is also a terrific . . . terrific preservative. Her head took two litres of Coca-Cola and a roll of masking tape to bind her right back up. The doctors said I saved her life because of my quick thinking, suggested to me a night course in basic brain surgery as I obviously had the knack for it and two years later . . . here I am!

BLAKE AS VERA (*she's not convinced*). That's quite a story.

DINNY. It certainly is.

SEAN *re-enters from the wardrobe as his seven-year-old self.*

SEAN. All right we play in the back garden, Dad?

DINNY. Yes, Sean. Where's Blake?

BLAKE. Here, Dad.

DINNY. I want you to stay out there for the afternoon and look after your little brother, all right, Blake?!

BLAKE (*in awe*). This place is beautiful.

DINNY (*growling*). Outside outside!

BLAKE *and* SEAN *run and enter a wardrobe.*

DINNY *looks very agitated.*

BLAKE AS VERA *and* SEAN AS PADDY *re-enter.*

SEAN AS PADDY. The little devils.

DINNY. Copper, all right?

SEAN AS PADDY. He was crying a little bit.

DINNY. They're feisty boys, them! Take after their old man.

SEAN AS PADDY. Little tearaways you mean.

DINNY. Tearaways! Not at all.

BLAKE AS VERA. The way they acted in mass.

DINNY. Giddy that's all.

BLAKE AS VERA. They set fire to a nun, Dinny.

DINNY. In fairness, they didn't know it was a nun. She frightened the life out of them, that's all.

BLAKE AS VERA. She was in a terrible state.

DINNY. Arrah she was put out wasn't she . . . eventually.

SEAN AS PADDY. You shouldn't have given them those Mars Bars earlier.

BLAKE AS VERA. Church is no place for Mars Bars, Dinny.

>BLAKE *enters the kitchen and changes into* MAUREEN*'s wig*.

DINNY. No place is no place for Mars Bars, Vera. The fact is the Mars Bar's like eating shit on a stick. Worse . . . sure doesn't it rot your teeth.

>BLAKE AS MAUREEN *re-enters with Ryvita sandwiches on a plate*.

(*Announcing*.) Ahh sandwiches, great stuff, Maureen! My favourites aren't they?

>SEAN *looks very nervous*.

BLAKE AS MAUREEN. Spreadable cheddar, Dinny . . .

>DINNY *freezes when he sees them*.

DINNY. What's this?

BLAKE (*as himself*). Sandwiches, Dad.

DINNY. Ryvita sandwiches?

SEAN. There was no sliced pan in Tesco, Dad.

DINNY. Supermarket, isn't it?

SEAN. I know but . . .

DINNY. Didn't you go?

SEAN. I did, Dad.

DINNY. You didn't go.

SEAN. I did.

DINNY. Don't answer me back or I'll thump ya!

BLAKE. Maybe we –

DINNY. Shut up, you! The story calls for sliced pan bread, doesn't it?

SEAN. I know but –

DINNY. The story doesn't work if we don't have the facts and Ryvitas aren't the facts . . . they're not close to the facts. A batched loaf is close to the facts, a bread roll is closer still but a Ryvita? . . . A Ryvita's just taking the piss, Sean. A Ryvita's a great leap of the imagination.

BLAKE. It's the right cheese.

DINNY. Feck the cheese! It's sticking out like a sore thumb. Your mother would never make crispy sandwiches, would she? You two little boys playing out in the garden out there . . . you'll not be happy with Ryvita!

SEAN. I can go back to Tesco if you want.

DINNY. Ah forget about it. And another thing, don't be cutting corners, you!

SEAN. How'd you mean?

DINNY. 'London's a tough old nut. For a while I was working the sites but London's all grown up now and not much building for fellas like me.' Then what, then what?

SEAN. Truth is I haven't worked for six years . . .

DINNY. 'The truth be told the Irishman is not the master builder of yesteryear. That title belongs to the men of Eastern Europe. Built like buses they are. Feet like double beds. The truth is I haven't worked for six years, Dinny.'

SEAN. That's a new line, Dad.

DINNY. So?

SEAN. You want me to use it?

DINNY. Getting lazy on me?

SEAN. No, Dad.

DINNY. Sloppy, Sean.

SEAN. Sorry, Dad.

DINNY. You wanna get your act together. There'll be no chance of the actin' trophy gathering dust on your shelf if you don't pull up them socks, boy.

SEAN. Right, Dad.

DINNY (*pointing to the trophy*). The acting trophy, Sean!

SEAN. Yes, Dad.

DINNY. Acting trophy!

SEAN. I know, Dad.

DINNY. Blake, make your entrance.

> BLAKE *turns back into the kitchen. He sighs.*

BLAKE (*to himself*). Shite.

DINNY (*to* SEAN). We'll talk about this later, right?!

SEAN. All right, Dad.

> BLAKE AS MAUREEN *re-enters with the sandwiches.*

DINNY. Ahh sandwiches, great stuff! My favourites aren't they, Maureen?

BLAKE AS MAUREEN. Spreadable cheddar, Dinny.

DINNY. Ohh lovely! Rich and creamy.

> *He bites into the Ryvita sandwich but it crumbles all over the place. He grimaces and looks like he's about to explode but* SEAN *quickly continues the performance.*

SEAN AS PADDY. Terrible shock going all the way to the cemetery and not being able to stick Mammy in the ground.

DINNY. A disgrace.

SEAN AS PADDY. Whoever heard of a gravedigger without a digger. Like a postman without post, a brickie without bricks, a shopkeeper without a shop, a cook without a cooker, a footballer without a foot, a bus driver without a bus, a fishmonger without a fish –

BLAKE AS VERA (*stopping him*). Paddy!

SEAN AS PADDY. Awful though. You had every right to hit that gravedigger as we left for home, Dinny.

DINNY. Couldn't get up much speed in that hearse though.

SEAN AS PADDY. No.

DINNY. Still . . . I managed to reverse and have another pop off the little fecker. (*Laughs a little.*)

SEAN AS PADDY. Christ it's great to be back with the big brother! The brain surgeon living in the gaff on the hill overlooking Cork City in all its finery.

DINNY. And what news of London Town, Paddy? This Walworth Road off the Elephant and Castle, paint me a picture of this boulevard and its surrounding environs.

SEAN AS PADDY *clears his throat.*

SEAN AS PADDY. On my palate is only grey, Dinny.

DINNY. Right.

SEAN AS PADDY. Grey and muck. For these are the two primary colours that make up much of the Elephant.

DINNY. I see.

SEAN AS PADDY. And as for the Castle . . . not so much a fortress, for a billion cars daily circle this grassy knoll known as 'the roundabout'.

DINNY. 'Daily traverse'!

SEAN AS PADDY. For a billion cars daily *traverse* this grassy knoll known as 'the roundabout'.

DINNY. Better.

SEAN AS PADDY. A million tiny bedsits there are. Large carbuncles sprouting out from the ground. Massive flats. Deadly, pitiful places that even the rats have abandoned, the cockroaches have done cockroaching and all that's left is London people.

DINNY. Jaynee.

SEAN AS PADDY. To sum it up in pure Cork parlance . . . the place is a hole.

BLAKE AS VERA. The lot of London is, Dinny.

DINNY. You do often read stories that they do eat their young over there, Paddy and Vera. So criminal and violent they are that Londoners like nothing more than skinning an Irishman halfway through his drink.

SEAN AS PADDY. Sacrilegious, boy. Sacrilegious. (*He knocks back his can of beer.*)

BLAKE AS VERA. And what news of Cork City, Dinny?

DINNY. Well, Vera, my love, there she is laid out in front of us.

SEAN AS PADDY. Aw beautiful.

DINNY. Laid out in all her finery.

BLAKE AS VERA (*wistfully*). Ah Cork.

DINNY. I often do stand here after a long day brain-surgeoning and just drink in this wonderful sight with a fine glass of red wine and a packet of those green Pringles. For I liken Cork City to a large jewel, Paddy and Vera.

SEAN AS PADDY. Do ya?

DINNY. I do. A jewel with the majestic River Lee ambling through it, chopping the diamond in two before making its way to murkier climes . . . towards the poisonous Irish Sea for example. Ah yes, Cork City. You could call it Ireland's jewel but you'd be A FUCKING IDIOT, BOY. FOR IT IS, REALLY AND TRULY, IRELAND'S TRUE CAPITAL CITY.

SEAN *and* BLAKE *applaud.*

SEAN AS PADDY. Oh well said, Dinny!

DINNY. The red and the white, Paddy! The blood and the
bandage, little brother! Blood and the bandage!

BLAKE AS VERA. I'll help Maureen prepare the chicken.

BLAKE AS VERA *goes to the kitchen and opens the oven.
He nearly falls back in horror. He slams it shut immediately.*

SEAN AS PADDY. And Dinny, tell me, tell me . . . would
Mammy stand beside you and look at this very same view?

DINNY. She would, Paddy. She would. Me with my red wine,
her standing with a pint of Beamish in her hand.

SEAN AS PADDY (*smiling*). Ah yes.

DINNY. A bottle of Harp in her other hand.

SEAN AS PADDY. That's right.

DINNY. A large glass of whiskey by the coffee table.

SEAN AS PADDY. That's her.

DINNY. And a can of Heineken in her coat pocket.

SEAN AS PADDY. She loved her drink.

DINNY (*with admiration*). You know when they pulled that
horse off her, you could actually smell the whiskey from her
blood. I mean, that's incredible, boy.

SEAN AS PADDY. And I always thought it would be the drink
that would finally kill her.

DINNY. Well, it was in a way, Paddy. Those gooseberries she
was gathering were for fermenting in a lethal vat of alcohol
she called her 'Preservative'.

SEAN AS PADDY. Ohh the irony.

DINNY. I know, cruel, isn't it? (*Instructing him.*) 'So what
about the will, Dinny?!'

SEAN AS PADDY. So what about the will, Dinny?

DINNY (*snaps*). Jesus, Sean, quicker! Quicker!

SEAN AS PADDY. Did she mention to you what might be in the will?

DINNY *takes a moment, furious that* SEAN *has messed up. The two boys tense. Suddenly:*

DINNY. The will, she did, Paddy! She gave me a hint a few weeks ago. But as custom will have it, the will must be read with the wives present.

SEAN AS PADDY (*eagerly calling*). Vera, love, the will!

DINNY (*just as eager and rubbing his hands*). Maureen, sweetheart, the reading of the will.

BLAKE *comes running from the kitchen wearing* MAUREEN*'s wig and carrying* VERA*'s wig.*

The three enter the bedroom and surround the coffin.

Read it loud and clear, Maureen.

BLAKE *takes the will from a sealed envelope and reads it.*

BLAKE AS MAUREEN. 'To my loving sons Denis and Patrick.'

SEAN AS PADDY. Nice touch.

BLAKE AS MAUREEN. 'I'm on the bus back home from the pub and fairly tanked up so here's the will. As your father would say, you two boys were the only family we ever had, you weren't much but we loved you . . . though we never got around to showing it on account of the terrible poverty we were under.'

DINNY. That's true.

BLAKE AS MAUREEN. 'But as you know the house you grew up in is now worth a few bob and can be carved up between the both of you.

DINNY *clears his throat.*

However, it's my wish that the son who is the most sensible, the most successful with his own money, the most balanced in his own life, should act as executor of the estate.

DINNY *has started to smile and nod to himself.*

That son will organise a small allowance to be paid monthly into his brother's account so that he doesn't piss it up a wall.

DINNY *fails to suppress his laughter.*

(*Quickly.*) A memorandum of the special gifts I want divided between family members is listed below. All the best in life. The bus is stopped so that's me off to the chipper. Mammy.'

DINNY (*erupting*). Well, that's clear as clear!

SEAN AS PADDY. How d'you mean?

DINNY. Take a look around you, Paddy. A far cry from Walworth Road and its deserting rats, aren't we?

SEAN AS PADDY. Suppose.

DINNY. She had mentioned to me she was worried the money wouldn't be handled sensibly what with our histories. She's looking for a steady hand, you see.

BLAKE AS VERA. He's lying, he's lying, Paddy!

SEAN AS PADDY (*looking at the will*). He's not, Vera! That's Mammy's will all right. You can smell the Bushmills off it.

DINNY. Fear not, little brother. As controller of the estate and your yearly allowance I'll make sure things are completely transparent.

SEAN AS PADDY. Monthly allowance.

DINNY. In the meantime we can keep ourselves happy with the personal gifts left in the memorandum by Mammy. Maureen, sweetheart.

BLAKE AS MAUREEN (*reading*). 'My deep fat fryer for my son Denis.'

DINNY (*triumphantly*). Yes!

BLAKE AS MAUREEN. 'And three cans of Harp for Patrick.'

SEAN AS PADDY. Ah Jesus.

DINNY (*laughing*). Three cans of Harp! You always were her favourite. You need a hand basting that chicken, Maureen!?

DINNY *and* BLAKE AS MAUREEN *leave the bedroom and walk across to the kitchen.*

(*Still laughing.*) Jesus but it's working like a dream.

BLAKE AS MAUREEN (*distracted*). This house is beautiful.

DINNY (*laughing*). A brain surgeon!? Can you believe it?! We'll fill them with the roast chicken and get them on the car ferry back to London. A monthly allowance? He's got two chances . . . none and . . .

BLAKE *pulls a baking tray out of the oven with the huge salami sausage on it. Seeing it:*

(*Snaps and screams.*) SEAN!

SEAN. Coming, Dad!

SEAN *comes running from the bedroom towards the kitchen.* DINNY *grabs a large frying pan.*

DINNY (*growls to himself*). A fecking sausage!?

SEAN *enters and immediately* DINNY *swings the frying pan across the back of* SEAN*'s head.* SEAN *hits the floor fast.*

A long pause as DINNY *and* BLAKE *look at* SEAN *on the floor.*

DINNY *takes a cup of water and gargles a little. He then spits it out on* SEAN*'s head.*

(*To* BLAKE, *calmly.*) Get him up and sort him out.

DINNY *goes back into the living room and sits in the armchair. He takes his wig off. He takes up a massive bottle of moisturising cream, squeezes some in his hand and aggressively applies it to his face and head.*

BLAKE *helps* SEAN *up.*

SEAN *sits at the table and* BLAKE *stands.*

A long pause.

The two brothers talk in hushed tones.

BLAKE. Are you okay?

SEAN. Yeah.

A pause.

BLAKE. What's with the shopping?

SEAN. I picked up the wrong bag in Tesco. (*A pause.*) It was a mistake.

BLAKE *looks in at* DINNY.

What's he doing?

BLAKE. Puttin' on his cream.

BLAKE *faces into the kitchen.*

A long pause.

SEAN. Something else happened to me, Blake.

BLAKE. Did someone try to get ya?

SEAN. No. No one ever does. You should come out with me the next time.

BLAKE *doesn't respond.*

A pause.

DINNY *is smelling the contents of the biscuit tin again.*

BLAKE. When we came here as little kids you could still smell Ireland from our jumpers.

SEAN (*distantly*). Yeah.

BLAKE. You could smell Mammy's cooking, couldn't you? It was roast chicken that last day and it was a lovely smell, hey Sean? And I think we might have come across on a boat . . . (*Prompting* SEAN, *smiling.*) Go on.

BLAKE *holds* SEAN*'s hand.*

SEAN (*continuing*). And despite the sea and wind, the smell of Mammy's cooking and that chicken was still stuck in the wool of our jumpers.

BLAKE. And I can't remember getting off a boat . . . but maybe we got a bus then to London, Sean, and still Mammy right around us.

SEAN. And Dad must have locked the door as soon as we were inside because the smell sort of stayed longer.

BLAKE. And for a while it stayed and we must have talked about the chicken smell and we must have missed Mammy, hey Sean?

SEAN. Yeah, we must have.

BLAKE. Dad all talk of Ireland, Sean. Everything's Ireland. His voice is stuck in Cork so it's impossible to forget what Cork is. (*A pause.*) This story we play is everything. (*A pause.*) Once upon a time my head was full of pictures of Granny's coffin and Mr and Mrs Cotter and Paddy and Vera and Bouncer the dog and all those busy pictures in our last day. (*Smiling.*) 'Cause you'd say Dad's words and they'd give you pictures, wouldn't they, Sean? And so many pictures in your head . . . Sure you wouldn't want for the outside world even if it was a good world! You could be happy. (*A pause.*) But all them pictures have stopped. I say his words and all I can see is the word. A lot of words piled on top of other words. There's no sense to my day 'cause the sense isn't important anymore. No pictures. No dreams. Words only. (*A pause.*) All I've got is the memory of the roast chicken, Sean.

DINNY *enters the kitchen.*

DINNY. Explain the shopping to me then?

SEAN. A mistake, Dad.

DINNY. How a mistake?

SEAN. Someone tricked me with the wrong bag.

DINNY. Did they?

SEAN. Yes, Dad.

DINNY. Who?

SEAN. The girl at the cash register.

DINNY. Made fun of you, did she? Tricked you and then had a good laugh?

SEAN. She was a little bitch, Dad.

DINNY. She was a little bitch. And many more feckers out there, Sean, wanting to gobble you up.

SEAN. I can go back if you want.

DINNY. You're not enjoying going outside are you?

SEAN. Only if you want me to.

DINNY. Seems to me you might be enjoying it a little.

SEAN. No.

DINNY. Not like Blake here who knows he can't go out.

SEAN. I hate it too, Dad.

DINNY. Do you?

SEAN. I do.

DINNY. Are you lying to me about this girl that tricked you?

SEAN. No, Dad.

DINNY. 'Cause if you lie to me there'll be terrible trouble to pay.

SEAN. I know there will. There's no lying going on.

DINNY. Blake?

BLAKE. Yes, Dad.

DINNY. You're awful quiet.

BLAKE. Just keeping my energy. I know it's about to get real fast soon so just thinking things through again, that's all.

DINNY. Got your eyes on the actin' trophy, Blake? Such a prize.

BLAKE. Sure it's only you that gets to win it.

DINNY. But feck it, you're almost there, boy, almost.

BLAKE. Am I, Dad?

DINNY. You are. You've got the tough job playing the ladies, of course. (*Slight pause.*) Sort of nice playing Mammy though?

BLAKE. Yes, Dad.

DINNY. Christ she's a great woman, all right! A great woman! She'll be waiting in the kitchen back in Cork, lads! Waiting for her three men to walk back through the door.

BLAKE. When might that be, Dad? (*Slight pause.*) When?

DINNY *slowly inhales and announces loudly,*

DINNY. One day . . . ! One day!!

SEAN *races to the wardrobe.*

One day I'll buy a house just like this one, Maureen!

BLAKE *throws the sausage back in the oven and runs over and joins* SEAN *in the wardrobe.*

One day, by Jesus the Holy Christ, I'll live in a castle overlooking the banks of the lovely Lee. One day, mark my words! One day!

Large thumping noise and DINNY *is startled.*

By jaynee, who's this at the door?

SEAN *and* BLAKE *enter as Mr Cotter,* JACK, *and his brother-in-law* PETER *(both from Montenotte). They are carrying another cardboard coffin on their shoulders.*

BLAKE AS JACK. Watch the paintwork, Peter.

SEAN AS PETER. Sorry, Jack.

DINNY *freezes in the kitchen as he hears them.*

BLAKE AS JACK. I've just got a man in to do it for me actually. But by Jesus, what a day!

A gravedigger without a digger!? Have you ever heard of such shite.

SEAN AS PETER. Like a banker without a bank, a journalist without a journal, a painter without paint, a producer without produce, a publican without a pub, a zookeeper without a zoo . . .

BLAKE AS JACK. The list can go on, Peter, and we can just stand here with your dead father stuck in this box breaking my delicate little shoulders.

SEAN AS PETER. Well, it's your house, Jack, where do you want him?

BLAKE AS JACK. Stick him in the kitchen and out of my sight.

As they go into the kitchen, DINNY *runs out and across into the bedroom.*

BLAKE *and* SEAN *place the coffin down on the kitchen table.*

DINNY (*to himself*). By jaynee I wasn't expecting this at all! (*To* PADDY.) Back inside! Back inside! Look I'm sorry, Paddy, but they just called out of the blue. It wouldn't be appropriate to . . .

DINNY *has to wait for the two boys and is annoyed by this.*

(*Snapping.*) Move it, lads, for fuck sakes!

SEAN *exits the kitchen and runs over to the bedroom.* BLAKE *runs back to the wardrobe and enters it.*

SEAN AS PADDY. You're not going to introduce me to those men?

DINNY. It's business, Paddy.

SEAN AS PADDY. Brain-surgery business?

DINNY. That's right. Now I'll have to go out to my colleagues and talk to them, Paddy. Are you all right in here with these two lovely ladies?

SEAN AS PADDY. Three ladies, Dinny. Let's not forget Mammy just yet.

DINNY. You're right. (*Touching the coffin and sighing.*) Sorry, Paddy.

DINNY *turns away fast and exits the bedroom and into the sitting room at the same time as* BLAKE *enters from the wardrobe wearing a new woman's blonde permed wig. He plays the part of Mrs Cotter,* EILEEN.

BLAKE AS EILEEN (*upset*). Oh Denis!

DINNY. Yes Eileen.

BLAKE AS EILEEN. Where's the body, love?

DINNY. What?

BLAKE AS EILEEN. The coffin, Denis? The coffin.

DINNY. Well, let me explain first . . .

BLAKE AS EILEEN (*calls*). Peter!

DINNY (*to himself*). Shit shit!

> BLAKE AS EILEEN *enters the kitchen and throws his arms around the coffin.*

> DINNY *stands looking aghast at the coffin on the table.*

BLAKE AS EILEEN (*crying a little*). Did you know he slept in this box for two months before he . . . Like he had a premonition.

SEAN AS PETER. Really?

BLAKE AS EILEEN. He loved this box. And then to be struck down in his prime!

SEAN AS PETER. Daddy was ninety-six, Eileen.

BLAKE AS EILEEN. Take off the lid, I want to look at him.

> DINNY *stands in the sitting room listening to their conversation. They look into the coffin.*

SEAN AS PETER. Well, there he is. (*Slight pause.*) Bits of him, anyway.

BLAKE AS EILEEN. He went the way he would have liked to though, didn't he, Peter?

SEAN AS PETER. He did.

BLAKE AS EILEEN. Off the coast of Kinsale travelling at 140 miles an hour. The wind in his hair, his little sailor's outfit on. Speeding fast 'til he hits that bloody sea lion. (*Starts to cry.*) The speedboat thrown into the air. The boat travelling through that field, is that right?

SEAN AS PETER. That's right.

BLAKE AS EILEEN. The horse coming from nowhere. He hits the horse at 100-mile an hour sending it careering over a hedge and onto a quiet country road . . .

DINNY *faints from the shock and hits the ground hard.*

Denis!?

SEAN AS PETER. Good God! Is he all right? Who is he anyway?

BLAKE AS EILEEN. Our painter-decorator.

DINNY *comes around.*

Are you all right, Denis pet?

DINNY (*distantly*). Mother . . .

BLAKE AS EILEEN. No, it's me, Eileen.

DINNY. Horse.

BLAKE AS EILEEN. No, I'm not a horse.

DINNY. Mother . . . killed . . . horse.

BLAKE AS EILEEN. No Denis, that's not right, love. Daddy killed horse.

SEAN AS PETER. And horse killed Daddy.

BLAKE AS EILEEN. Help him into the chair, Peter, quick.

DINNY *is 'unconscious' in the armchair as* SEAN AS PETER *and* BLAKE AS JACK *have a covert conversation.*

BLAKE AS JACK. Is Eileen . . .?

SEAN AS PETER. She's in the kitchen looking at Daddy again.

BLAKE AS JACK. Well, what a complete waste of time.

SEAN AS PETER. I know, I know!

BLAKE AS JACK. Filling him with drink, sticking him on that speedboat and to what end?!

SEAN AS PETER. Well, perhaps Eileen has his money? She could have taken it somewhere, couldn't she?

BLAKE AS JACK. I know my wife's face. She knew that your father kept his money in his house but this morning when we turned everything upside down and found nothing! Her face, Peter?! She was devastated, boy!

He takes a can of beer from SEAN AS PETER*'s hands and finishes it.*

SEAN AS PETER. Well, he'd hardly have gotten rid of it, would he?

DINNY *gets up from the armchair and goes to enter the bedroom as* SEAN AS PADDY *tries to exit the bedroom.*

DINNY. What the hell are you doing!?

SEAN AS PADDY. I have to go to the toilet.

DINNY. You can't.

SEAN AS PADDY. I'm bursting!

DINNY. You'll have to do it in there.

SEAN AS PADDY. It's a dining room!

DINNY. Out the window then.

SEAN AS PADDY. In front of the girls?

SEAN *exits the other door and appears in the living room as* PETER.

SEAN AS PETER. Are they your children out there?

DINNY. What?

SEAN AS PETER. In the garden. They're on the putting green outside.

BLAKE AS JACK *walking fast towards the wardrobe.*

BLAKE AS JACK. My putting green, the little shits!

He enters the wardrobe.

SEAN AS PETER. And I've seen some people inside the dining room.

DINNY *freezes*.

BLAKE AS EILEEN *re-enters the living room and heads for the kitchen*.

From the back garden. A man and two women, don't deny it now!

BLAKE AS EILEEN *pulls out the sausage in the pan*.

BLAKE AS EILEEN (*calling, confused*). Denis, love, what is this?

DINNY. Yes, Mrs Cotter.

BLAKE as EILEEN *brings the large sausage and pan inside to the living room*.

BLAKE AS EILEEN. Is this your chicken?

DINNY. I thought you might fancy a little bit of roast chicken after the funeral.

SEAN AS PETER. How did you know we were coming back? You couldn't have possibly known we were going to arrive back this afternoon. You've been eating Eileen and Jack's food, haven't you? (*He grabs the sausage*.) There's nothing you'd like more than having your three friends around, drinking someone else's alcohol and feeding yourselves with somebody else's chicken . . .

DINNY *screams. He grabs the large sausage and flings it against the wall. It disintegrates*.

Long pause as SEAN *and* BLAKE *brace themselves*.

DINNY (*quietly*). It's not working with the sausage. It's not right.

SEAN (*instinctively*). Is any of it?

Immediately, SEAN *regrets saying anything*. DINNY *grabs him by the hair*.

DINNY. What? Say it!

SEAN. Is any of this story real?

DINNY. Don't doubt me. We allow Mister Doubt into this flat and where would we be? Blake?

BLAKE. We'd be outside, Dad.

DINNY (*not liking* BLAKE'*s tone*). Are you getting brave on me too?

BLAKE. I think I might want to go back to Ireland now.

DINNY. Do I not care for you both? The two little boys who followed me over, didn't I take you in and feed you? Little scraps all tired and hungry, wasn't it me who took you in?

BLAKE. Yes, Dad.

DINNY *grabs* BLAKE *by the ear and drags him into the sitting room.* SEAN *stands at the kitchen entrance looking at them.*

DINNY. And the sea, Blake. The sea, the sea, the sea, the sea, the sea . . .

BLAKE. Dad, don't!

DINNY'*s delivery is focused and steady, he speaks it to* BLAKE.

DINNY. The sea it spits me out onto England. I stand on the shore with Ireland on my back and the tide pushing me across the land towards London. I run, Blake.

BLAKE. I know it, Dad.

DINNY. I run the same race a million Irishmen ran. But pockets full of new money and Paddy's keys in my hands with Walworth Road a final destination, a sure thing, a happy ever after. I run. I run right past the cars in the motorways, the trains in their tracks. I run fast towards London. Days and nights they merge into the one memory. Only the running has any matter. Countryside passing through me and a final farewell to the green. And no horizon of London, I see. No towers or flats or big gate to welcome Dinny. Just road signs and not grass under feet anymore but hard grey now. The road signs steering me. Like a little rat caught in a drain. Pushing me further and further to its centre. But what centre? Me and my suit rolling down the motorway with buildings tighter on either side. And tighter and tighter still, Blake, and when they

30

can't get any tighter, taller they grow. With each mile I run, higher they climb and smaller the dot. Higher the buildings and smaller me. I close my eyes from the size of this place. I stop. Stood still then. (*Long pause.*) The noise and running all stopped, Blake. And I'm stood on grass. I look down at my shoes all knackered . . . soles worn from the run. I catch my breath. I can hear my breathing. So it's all quiet, you see. Ssshhhhhhh. (*A pause.*) I smell the roast chicken from my jumper, Blake. Your mother's kiss to me at the door and telling me, 'Leave now.' (*Slight pause.*) And I think of Paddy and Vera. Their little poisoned bodies piled up on the floor back in Mrs Cotter's house in Cork City. And then I think of me and Paddy as children back in the good old days. A day trip to Robert's Cove and Paddy runs into the sea, a big wave taking him, Dad lost in the pub and I wade in and pick the toddler up. It's only a little bit of water we stand in but Paddy's crying like a scared baba. I take him out and wrap him in Dad's towel. I keep him warm, you know. And I feel good when I think of me and the love I have for Paddy. I stand there looking at the green scabby grass of the roundabout and my knackered shoes. Fuck. (*A pause.*) And then what happened, Blake? What then, tell me?

BLAKE *continues, detached.*

BLAKE. And then it starts from the tiniest quiet thing. You can feel the little shakes up through the grass and up through your body now. Noises from the outside start filling you up. Loud car noises. Stood still with cars all wrapped around your head, stood in the middle of the Elephant and the Castle with Walworth Road right there in front of you. Walworth Road and Paddy and Vera's flat. Only the road to run and get inside, to get you safe. You run fast, Dad.

His eyes suddenly fill with tears. He's terrified.

And then the people. They come out from houses and shops and they're after you. Their skin, it falls to the ground and them bodies running you down and wanting to tear you to shreds. From the river they're coming. They come up from the ground. The concrete snaps open and the bodies are up

fast. And they're all snapping teeth and grabbing hands they have. Run faster and faster until a thousand green windows reaching up into the sky and Paddy's flat right at the top and it's calling you. Take to the stairs with the other flats teeming out the bodies wanting to grab you down and get ya. The stairs and your speed. Further away from them you move as you climb higher and the flat higher still. Further away they fall as the flat still higher.

BLAKE *can't continue*.

DINNY. And then, Sean?

SEAN. At cloud height you are and looking over all of London with its bodies down below, its tighter-than-tight buildings, its chewed-up grey, them bad people calling you down. In Paddy and Vera's flat and you're looking over all them who want to gobble us up 'til we're no more. Inside and your heart begins to slow now that you have these safe walls. (*A pause*.) At the window and you're looking out past the end of Walworth Road, past where London stretches into the green countryside, past the green and over the sea to Ireland and to Cork and past the River Lee and high up into the estate and our little terraced house. (*Slight pause*.) And there's Mammy standing by the sink washing the dishes in the kitchen. From the window you can see all of this. In Paddy's flat and you're safe.

Long pause. DINNY *embraces* BLAKE.

DINNY. You believe that lie about that cash-register girl tricking Sean?

BLAKE *doesn't answer*. SEAN *looks on*. DINNY *looks at* SEAN *as he holds* BLAKE.

One lie leads to the next and pretty soon them bodies from outside be banging down our door and dragging you down below, Blake. You watch Sean for me, all right?

BLAKE *turns away and walks into the kitchen*.

SEAN *follows him inside*.

DINNY *sits down and begins to moisturise his head and face again*.

When BLAKE *enters the kitchen he goes straight to a drawer and takes out a large kitchen knife.*

SEAN *watches him.*

BLAKE *faces the sitting room ready to re-enter. The knife is meant for* DINNY.

BLAKE. Them bodies won't get us if we leave the flat, Sean?

SEAN. London's not the way he tells it.

BLAKE. You're sure of it? 'Cause I'm ready to finish it, Sean, but you're sure we won't be got by anyone outside?

SEAN. Well, today I spoke to someone.

BLAKE *turns to him.*

A girl in Tesco, Blake. Got all our food and paid her. She knows me 'cause I'm in at ten o'clock every morning getting the same food for the story. She says that she's seen where I live. Asks me what I do. I can't tell her the truth of what we do in here all day so I say that I'm a builder, though I'm no builder. She's talked about Ireland and how she's seen it on the telly, Blake. She talks about the funny colour of the grass and then the sea. I tell her that I like the sea but how I hadn't seen the sea in so long and she says, 'I'll take you to Brighton Beach and we can walk there.' She means it. She definitely means to take me to that place. So I leave sort of in a daze 'cause of the way she talked to me. I picked up the wrong shopping bag and didn't get out of the daze until I got back here and saw that fecking sausage. But her talking to me like that, Blake . . . even besides the great thing she said . . . her just talking so nice to me . . . it got me thinking more than ever . . . It's right that us two leave.

A pause. BLAKE*'s face hardens. He's not happy.*

BLAKE. You talked to someone outside?

SEAN. She's called Hayley.

They suddenly hear 'A Nation Once Again' sung by Paddy Reilly blasting from the tape recorder.

SEAN *walks through the living room through to the bedroom and takes up his position.*

BLAKE *violently slams the knife into the kitchen table.*

He stares angrily in at SEAN.

He enters the living room as EILEEN *and takes up his position.*

Everything as it should be, DINNY *turns off the music.*

BLAKE AS EILEEN. Can you explain this to me, Dinny?

DINNY. I can, Eileen, I can.

SEAN AS PADDY *enters the sitting room fast and races towards the wardrobe.*

SEAN AS PADDY. Sorry, Dinny, but the bladder's packed it in finally!

He enters the wardrobe.

BLAKE AS EILEEN. Who was that?

DINNY. My brother.

BLAKE *enters the bedroom and re-enters the sitting room as* VERA *and walks right across and into the kitchen and picks up a plate of Ryvita sandwiches.*

SEAN AS PETER *re-enters.*

SEAN AS PETER. So that's your brother in the toilet. Who was that?

DINNY. His wife.

SEAN AS PETER. And what is she doing here?

BLAKE as VERA *re-enters with the Ryvita sandwiches.*

BLAKE AS VERA. Just passing around these lovely sandwiches. I know you people could go a whole day without eating, just thinking those heady thoughts with no time for your stomachs. Didn't imagine that Dinny here would find himself in such illustrious company.

SEAN *goes back to the wardrobe.*

BLAKE AS EILEEN. And you made these sandwiches . . . ?

BLAKE AS VERA. Vera. No I didn't actually make them, no. It was Maureen.

BLAKE AS EILEEN. And who's she?

BLAKE AS VERA. Oh she's Dinny's wife!

BLAKE AS EILEEN. And is she . . . ?

BLAKE AS VERA. She's in the dining room, yeah. Sure I'll just get her for ya.

SEAN AS PETER *re-enters*.

SEAN AS PADDY. Well, thank God for that. Had an awful premonition that my hole would finally strike and I'd be lying prostrate on that lovely bathroom floor of yours. Well then!

DINNY. Eileen, this is Paddy the brother and my wife Maureen.

SEAN AS PADDY. Doctor.

BLAKE AS EILEEN. I beg your pardon?

SEAN AS PADDY. Is there a collective term for brain surgeons?

BLAKE AS EILEEN. I've no idea.

SEAN AS PADDY. You know Dinny here was thrown out of school when he was fifteen for smearing a school desk with . . .

DINNY. Thanks for that, Paddy.

SEAN AS PETER. Quite a gathering. With so many people helping surely your little job in the dining room is finished, Denis?

BLAKE AS VERA. What's there to do apart from sit around and grieve. The sandwiches are made, the chicken is cooking. We all just have to settle into a long evening of drinking. Drinking to life and toasting to death.

SEAN AS PETER. Well, that's very kind of you, Vera. It shows a beautiful character. Someone who can reach out to a stranger who's lost a parent.

BLAKE AS VERA (*covertly*). Can you see that?

SEAN AS PETER. Well, it's obvious.

BLAKE AS VERA. A stranger really?

SEAN AS PETER. Of course.

BLAKE AS VERA. You're right, you know. Do you think in eight years of marriage a person can end up a stranger with their own husband?

SEAN AS PETER. Well, that's an altogether different matter.

DINNY (*in mid-conversation*). . . . and Maureen knowing of this imminent gathering thought to prepare some finger food for us all.

BLAKE AS EILEEN. Maureen, that's very kind of you.

DINNY. Kind? Sure she lives for the kitchen!

BLAKE AS EILEEN. Even somebody else's kitchen, Maureen?

A pause as BLAKE AS MAUREEN *looks flustered.*
DINNY *thrown.*

BLAKE AS MAUREEN. I'll get on with that chicken so!

DINNY. Great stuff, Maureen! Thanks, love.

BLAKE AS MAUREEN *walks into the kitchen, sees the open coffin and audibly gasps.*

DINNY *races into her.*

BLAKE AS MAUREEN (*whispering*). How did Mammy get over here?

DINNY. That's not Mammy. It's Mrs Cotter's father, look.

BLAKE AS MAUREEN (*looking inside*). What's he doing there?

DINNY. What do you think?! He's dead. Now stay put and cook, Maureen. Cook your little heart out! Get people's mouths full and they won't be able to speak, right.

DINNY *exits into the sitting room.*

BLAKE *exits into the stage right wardrobe.*

SEAN AS PADDY. Lovely people, Dinny! You'd imagine brain surgeons all stuffy. But nothing like it. She's lovely, Eileen! Said you were a great worker and that I could learn a lot from you . . . 'Though one brain surgeon in the family is enough, thank you very much, Eileen!' And look how that Peter fella's chatting up my Vera and getting close to her. Real charming bunch, aren't they? Christ it's shaping up into a lovely day!

BLAKE AS JACK *enters through the wardrobe.*

BLAKE AS JACK. Are these your two little boys, Denis!?

DINNY. Well, that depends, Mr Cotter . . .

BLAKE AS JACK. I walk out to the garden and they've got a neighbourhood child, Finbarr, pinned to the putting green. A great big bloody arm on him, Eileen. He's spread-eagled and knocked unconscious by these two little brats who are just about to do the unspeakable.

DINNY. Blake, explain this to me now?! Sean, come on.

SEAN. He was all by himself with his dog Bouncer and we thought it would be fun if he played with us.

BLAKE. Finbarr's in the scouts and came back with his tent so we could play soldiers.

SEAN. He told us about survival and how he was being trained to survive in the wild.

DINNY. What age is this boy?

BLAKE. Six.

DINNY. Carry on.

SEAN. So he's bragging, Dad. He's bragging about surviving in the wild, about pissing on snake bites when a snake does bite. And all this time he's unpacking his tent.

BLAKE. No tent in there, Dad. Just poles and pins.

SEAN. So I says that maybe he should be the tent. Maybe we should pin down Finbarr and stick a pole up his centre and keep cover under him.

BLAKE. We pin him down and he starts to cry like a baby and not the bush man he makes himself out to be. Sets his big dog on us. Now Sean's afraid of dogs, that's right, isn't it, Dad?

DINNY. He is, yeah.

BLAKE. So I pick up a pole and start on Bouncer to protect my little brother.

DINNY. Good man, Blake.

BLAKE. Give him a few whacks on the back and he's getting fierce angry.

SEAN. And all the time we're sort of dancing over 'Finbarr the tent' on the ground. When all of a sudden . . .

BLAKE. Snap!

SEAN. Terrible noise, Dad.

BLAKE. I look down and see Finbarr's little arm in Bouncer's mouth.

SEAN. He's only six so he's got every right to fall unconscious, Dad.

BLAKE. I take the tent pole and one last swipe, I fire it right up Bouncer's arse. He's away like a bat of hell with the pole still dangling out his rear end and here we are with Finbarr's bloody arm needing some serious attention.

SEAN. Well, all this talk of being out in the wild and surviving on the basics and what we did next just seemed liked the most natural.

BLAKE. Looking at his broken arm we decided to give it the snake bite treatment.

SEAN. So we pissed on him.

A pause.

DINNY *turns to 'the others' and shrugs his shoulders.*

DINNY. Fair play.

SEAN *enters the kitchen as* PETER.

BLAKE *enters the kitchen as* JACK.

BLAKE AS JACK (*furiously*). For Christ's sake, Peter. We shouldn't have bothered murdering this old shit.

He grabs a can beer from SEAN*'s hand.*

SEAN AS PETER. Keep your voice down, Jack.

BLAKE AS JACK *drains the can of beer, much to* SEAN AS PETER*'s annoyance.*

BLAKE AS JACK. For all his money your father's worthless to us. This coffin is worth more than him.

BLAKE AS JACK *pulls up the pillow.*

This ridiculous plump lining.

He starts to bang the pillow off the coffin.

Jesus the extravagance of the man. This silk bloody pillow with his initials on it for GOD'S SAKE!! I MEAN . . .

Suddenly the pillow tears and Monopoly money is thrown in the air.

Suddenly the doorbell makes a continuous buzzing sound.

The three of them freeze.

The doorbell stops.

Instinctively, BLAKE *grabs a kitchen knife to protect himself.*

BLAKE *and* SEAN *come out to the sitting room and look at the front door.*

The doorbell sounds again.

BLAKE *and* SEAN *look to their father. He points to* BLAKE *to open it.*

With huge trepidation BLAKE *walks towards the front door and begins to undo the many locks.*

He then opens the door and steps way back as he holds the kitchen knife.

It's raining outside and standing in the rain is a twenty-four-year-old black woman holding a Tesco bag.

The three just stare at her.

This is HAYLEY.

HAYLEY (*hesitantly*). Is Sean in? It's just he took the wrong shopping. This is his one.

The three just look at her.

HAYLEY *then recognises* SEAN.

Hey Sean! It's me, Hayley.

SEAN *wants to disappear. He looks at the floor.*

She enters out of the rain. BLAKE *moves back from her.*

A pause.

Hey.

DINNY. Is there a cooked chicken and sliced pan in there?

HAYLEY. Yeah. And two packets of pink wafers and . . . well what you usually get.

A pause.

DINNY. Can you cook?

HAYLEY. Why? Is this like *Ready Steady Cook* or something?! Only you don't look like Ainsley Harriott!

She laughs.

DINNY *just stares through her and waits for her to stop laughing.*

She stops laughing.

DINNY. Can you cook?

HAYLEY *a little awkward now.*

HAYLEY. Yeah.

HAYLEY *stands as the three just stare at her for a long time and the rain continues outside.*

Loud guttural rhythmic music fades up and fills the stage and auditorium.

The music continues to build, the stage reverberating and unable to take its noise.

Blackout.

Silence.

Curtain Falls.

End of Act One.

ACT TWO

The curtain rises quickly.

DINNY *stands in the centre of the sitting room staring towards the kitchen.*

BLAKE *stands near him also looking towards the kitchen where* HAYLEY *and* SEAN *are talking.*

The nervous and talkative HAYLEY *has her coat off and wears a Tesco uniform.*

SEAN*'s naturally very anxious about her being inside their flat.*

HAYLEY*'s staring into the coffin.*

HAYLEY. That's a big box. What are you using it for? Looks like a coffin.

SEAN. It's just cardboard.

HAYLEY. I tell you, after them stairs, I could climb right in there for a little nap. What we up here? Fourteen floors . . .

SEAN. Fifteen.

HAYLEY. Fifteen floors with no lift! You should get on to the Council. Took me ten minutes to get up. I'm a pretty fit girl. I play football down Burgess Park. Well try . . . I'm not bad . . . But the important thing is to keep healthy. Do you do anything to keep fit?

SEAN (*distracted*). I do a bit of running.

HAYLEY. You get a decent workout from those stairs. Every morning at ten o'clock, up with your shopping.

SEAN. Yeah.

DINNY *gestures to* BLAKE *to pay attention to* HAYLEY.

BLAKE *stands by the kitchen entrance looking inside at her.*

HAYLEY. A creature of habit, aren't you? Oven-cooked chicken, white sliced bread, yeah? . . . Creamy milk, two packets of pink wafers, six cans of Harp and one cheesy spread. The other girls think you're an idiot but I was saying that there's a lot of sense to it. All the options that people have these days . . . it's all very confusing. If you're happy with your lifestyle and what you eat, why change?

During the following exchange, BLAKE *begins to mimic* HAYLEY*'s gestures, walk, stance. He's practising being her.*

Unaware of this, HAYLEY *suddenly notices the money on the kitchen floor.*

Is that Monopoly money?

SEAN. Yeah.

HAYLEY. Lively game was it? A bit messy in here. Is it just the three of you? Your brother and dad and you. No mother?

SEAN. She lives in Ireland.

HAYLEY. Divorced are they?

SEAN. No.

HAYLEY. Won't she come over? Doesn't she like London?

SEAN. I don't know.

HAYLEY. When you last see her?

SEAN. When I was five.

HAYLEY. Shut up! That's terrible. Five, really? Christ. Gotta get back and see her, Sean. Do you miss her?

SEAN. Yeah.

HAYLEY. Is she nice?

SEAN. She's a good cook.

HAYLEY. Aw you miss her cooking. How sweet. Why's your brother dressed like that?

SEAN. Like what?

HAYLEY. Like a woman. He's a transvestite, right?

SEAN. Ah what?

HAYLEY. He likes women's clothes.

SEAN. No it's a joke. He's just joking, that's all.

HAYLEY. I wouldn't mind if he was a transvestite.

SEAN. He's not.

HAYLEY. Well, I wouldn't mind if he was. It's a free world.

SEAN. He's a joker.

HAYLEY. He's a builder as well is he?

SEAN. Yeah a builder.

HAYLEY. So no building work today? Just chilling out?
Playing Monopoly. Taking it easy. Fooling around.

SEAN. Yeah.

HAYLEY. And dressing up in women's clothes?!

SEAN. Just Blake.

HAYLEY. The joker.

SEAN *looks back to the sitting room.*

Didn't know you were bald by the way. You always wear
that cute hat all the time. Looks like you shave it too. Is it a
fashion statement or something 'cause I quite like bald men.
Trying to impress me?

She laughs a little. She's flirting with him.

Sorry I'm talking so much. My mum reckons it's from
working at Tesco. You talk all day to the customers, get
home and I can't stop talking. It's not intentional! You get
stuck in a pattern. Christ, you've no idea what I mean, do
you?

SEAN. No I know what you mean.

HAYLEY. So was he serious? Your dad. He really wants me to
fix his lunch the way he said?

SEAN. He does, yeah.

HAYLEY. A bit rich though isn't it? I'm on my lunch break, I come up here as a favour and end up fixing his lunch.

SEAN. You've been very nice.

HAYLEY. Well, that's the Tesco training. It's all about customer care.

SEAN. Thank you.

HAYLEY. Thank you and have a nice day!

SEAN (*confused*). Okay.

HAYLEY. S'pose if I might get something out of it though?

She takes a can of Harp out of the Tesco bag and smiles.

A bit early but . . . after them stairs and . . .

She opens the can of beer.

DINNY *fires a look over at the kitchen as he hears the can open.*

HAYLEY *drinks some beer.*

BLAKE *does a perfect impersonation of* HAYLEY.

BLAKE. Looks like you shave it too. Are you trying to impress me?

HAYLEY *quickly turns and sees* BLAKE *looking in at her. She's a little nervous of him.*

HAYLEY. Very good. (*As* SEAN *takes her to one side.*) Why's he looking at me like that?

SEAN. Be honest with me please. Why did you come here?

A pause.

HAYLEY. To be nice. To do a nice thing.

A pause.

SEAN (*anxious*). But for no other reason, Hayley? Something you won't tell me?

HAYLEY. How d'you mean?

SEAN. Not to trick me?

HAYLEY's a little confused. She just laughs.

HAYLEY. Seriously?

DINNY puts on the tape recorder and 'An Irish Lullaby' begins to play.

SEAN tenses up. It can only mean one thing.

(*Of the music.*) That sounds nice. Quite old fashioned but I quite like that. (*Slight pause. Closes her eyes.*) Green grass. Stone walls. A little thatched cottage by the river. Little girl with red hair in ringlets sat on a donkey. (*Opening her eyes.*) Does it remind you of back home in Ireland?

SEAN. No.

A pause. She can see that SEAN looks frightened of something.

HAYLEY. I'm not here to trick you, Sean, honest.

She tugs at his sleeve playfully.

All right?

Seeing this, BLAKE enters fast and takes SEAN by the hand in an act of possession.

HAYLEY backs away from them.

Well, I suppose I'll get his lunch on then.

The music continues.

HAYLEY prepares the lunch.

DINNY stands up and puts his wig back on and grooms himself in preparation.

BLAKE gathers up the Monopoly money, refills and resets the pillow into the coffin.

SEAN looks terrified.

Suddenly DINNY slams the tape recorder off.

BLAKE and SEAN race into the sitting room.

The Farce resumes with pace. BLAKE *and* SEAN *are playing their younger selves.*

BLAKE. He's away like a bat of hell with the pole still dangling out his rear end and here we are with Finbarr's bloody arm needing some serious attention, Dad.

SEAN (*lowering his voice so* HAYLEY *doesn't hear*). Well all this talk of being out in the wild and surviving on the basics and what we did next just seemed the most natural.

BLAKE. Looking at his broken arm we decided to give it the snake bite treatment.

SEAN. So we pissed on him.

DINNY. Fair play.

BLAKE *grabs* SEAN *and quickly enters the kitchen with him.*

HAYLEY *turns to them.*

HAYLEY. D'you have any salt?

BLAKE AS JACK (*furious*). For Christ's sake, Peter. We shouldn't have bothered murdering this old shit.

He takes a can of beer from SEAN*'s hand.*

SEAN AS PETER. Keep your voice down, Jack.

BLAKE AS JACK (*draining the can of beer*). For all his money your father's worthless to us. This coffin is worth more than him.

BLAKE *pulls up the pillow.*

This ridiculous plump lining.

BLAKE *starts banging the pillow off the coffin.*

HAYLEY. Sean?

BLAKE AS JACK. Jesus the extravagance of the man. This silk bloody pillow with his initials on it for GOD'S SAKE!! I MEAN . . .

The pillow rips.

SEAN, BLAKE *and* HAYLEY *freeze as the Monopoly money falls around them.*

HAYLEY (*smiling*). Is this some sort of joke?

BLAKE *pulls* SEAN'*s arm and drags him back into the sitting room.*

DINNY. All right, boys, back in the back garden and behave yourself.

SEAN *and* BLAKE *disappear into the right wardrobe and reappear fast as* PADDY *and* EILEEN.

SEAN AS PADDY. Christ, Dinny, they're a handful, them kids. They wouldn't be my idea of children now.

HAYLEY *stands at the kitchen entrance. She's beginning to laugh at what's happening.*

DINNY. They wouldn't?

SEAN AS PADDY. I'd be of the thinking that children should be seen and not heard. Unless of course it was a children's choral choir in which case seeing and hearing would be an absolute delight.

HAYLEY *laughs a little.*

DINNY. Not at all, Paddy. Sure look at us. Raucous were we not? More than a handful. Two handfuls.

BLAKE AS EILEEN (*dreamily*). Bit of fighter were you, Denis?

DINNY. I was, Eileen. Back in the days when Cork City was dog rough, where to take a night-time stroll was an act of madness comparable to forcing long deadly skewers into your eyeballs, Cork was a jungle back then. And I'm not saying that I was its Tarzan . . .

SEAN AS PADDY. Because you can't swim.

DINNY. That's right, you're right. But I was more in the mode of King Kong, if you get my meaning. A gigantic freakish gorilla, intent on protecting his own and causing untold damage and chaos to those who challenge my jungle authority.

SEAN *looks towards* HAYLEY.

HAYLEY (*smiling*). It's good.

BLAKE AS EILEEN *gets closer to* DINNY.

BLAKE AS EILEEN (*whispering*). If only Jack had the same primal strength, the same domination.

DINNY (*whispering*). I know in this hour of grief I must be a symbol of reliability and power to you, Eileen. But I must warn you . . . flattery will get you into everywhere.

DINNY *and* BLAKE AS EILEEN *share a flirtatious laugh.*

BLAKE *and* SEAN *enter the kitchen fast, making* HAYLEY *step back into it.*

BLAKE AS JACK (*picking up the money*). How much do you think is here, Peter?

SEAN AS PETER. All of it maybe. These are big notes, Jack.

BLAKE AS JACK. Get it back in the coffin quick.

They gather up the money and shove it in the coffin.

HAYLEY. Can you stop just for a sec . . .

SEAN AS PETER. So what's our plan, Jack?

BLAKE AS JACK. Plan, plan, plan?! He stays here tonight. Tomorrow, me and you get him back in the hearse and drive. We pull over in a lay-by, divide the cash and get on with our new lives. Feck it, the sooner I leave that Eileen bitch and start to express myself the better!

SEAN AS PETER. Ah now that's my sister you're talking about, Jack.

BLAKE AS JACK. Oh the family man, are ya?! Filling your daddy with two bottles of gin, a bag of glue and strapping him into that speedboat, remember!

BLAKE AS JACK *grabs his beer and knocks it back.*

SEAN AS PETER (*peeved*). Why do you keep on taking my drink like that!?

DINNY (*explaining to* HAYLEY). Greedy Jack always hungry for the drink! Snatching it away at the last moment. Good detail, lads! We'll explain that in the finish! (*Prompting*.) Again, Blake, again!

BLAKE AS JACK. Filling your daddy with two bottles of gin, a bag of glue and strapping him into that speedboat, remember!

BLAKE AS JACK *grabs his beer and knocks it back*.

SEAN AS PETER (*peeved*). Why do you keep on taking my drink like that!?

DINNY. Excellent, boys!

BLAKE AS MAUREEN. Is everyone going to have chicken?

SEAN AS PETER *and* BLAKE AS JACK (*a scream*). Ahhh!

HAYLEY (*annoyed*). Helloooooooo!

BLAKE AS JACK (*whispering*). Who the hell's that?

SEAN AS PETER (*whispering*). The painter's wife, Maureen.

BLAKE AS JACK. Shit. Shit! (*Addressing* MAUREEN.) How much of that did you hear, Maureen?

BLAKE AS MAUREEN. Hearse. Lay-by. Dividing the cash.

BLAKE AS JACK. Well, it is ours.

BLAKE AS MAUREEN. What about Mrs Cotter?

SEAN AS PETER. Her husband Jack here's looking after her share.

HAYLEY. Right, I'm off then, Sean!

BLAKE AS JACK. It's not like it's any of your business anyway, Maureen.

HAYLEY. Sean!

SEAN AS PETER. It'll be our little secret then, Maureen?

BLAKE AS MAUREEN. I'll get on with the food so.

Irritated, HAYLEY *grabs her coat and bag and leaves the kitchen and heads for the front door.*

DINNY *looks at her as she tries to open the locks on the door.*

HAYLEY (*exasperated*). Oh open the fucking door!

DINNY *suddenly pounces on her and grabs her by the throat, pinning her to the door. He takes her bag and throws it to one side.*

SEAN *and* BLAKE *come out from the kitchen and stand by, watching.*

DINNY. Don't scream now.

HAYLEY, *terrified, looks towards* SEAN.

Here to break us up, boys. Trick us and drag us down to the street.

HAYLEY (*quietly*). What?

DINNY. Just do what I asked and you won't be hurt.

HAYLEY'*s eyes fill with tears.*

HAYLEY. But what are you doing?

A pause.

Why are you all doing this?

A pause as DINNY *just looks at her.*

DINNY. You be a good girl, take off your coat and do what I asked ya.

BLAKE *helps her off with her coat and immediately puts it on. Again he perfectly impersonates her.*

BLAKE. Thank you and have a nice day!

HAYLEY (*to* SEAN). Do something, Sean!

DINNY *turns* SEAN *towards him.*

DINNY. 'Feck it, Dinny, I don't . . .'

SEAN. Dad, please . . .

DINNY. 'Feck it, Dinny . . .'

SEAN. We can't keep her like this!

BLAKE. SAY IT, SEAN! SAY IT!

BLAKE and DINNY *side by side wait for* SEAN *to get back on track.*

SEAN *looks back at* HAYLEY.

HAYLEY. Please.

Then, slowly:

SEAN AS PADDY. Feck it, Dinny, I don't like that Peter fella at all! Closer he's getting to my Vera and the way he's looking down at me . . .

DINNY. Easy, Paddy. It's a walk in the garden you need.

HAYLEY *walks back into the kitchen as the three just look at her.*

Again, Sean! Come on! Come on!

SEAN AS PADDY (*more energy*). Feck it, Dinny, I don't like that Peter fella at all! Closer he's getting to my Vera and the way he's looking down at me . . .

DINNY. Easy, Paddy. It's a walk in the garden you need.

SEAN AS PADDY. I understand the stress you brain surgeons are under but I don't see you patronising me like that.

DINNY. Good man, Sean!

SEAN AS PADDY. You're not embarrassed of me are you?

DINNY. What?

BLAKE *takes off* HAYLEY*'s coat and drops it on the floor. He stands at the kitchen entrance looking in at her.*

SEAN AS PADDY. Embarrassed of me. Tell me straight, are ya, Dinny?

DINNY. Embarrassed of you? Embarrassed of my own little brother? A man who lives in abject poverty in a hovel in London. A brother so ugly that when he was born, the doctors thought our mother had pushed out her perforated poisoned liver. A man who as a boy was so unpopular that even his imaginary friends would beat him up. A brother so

stupid that for twenty years he thought that Irish dancing was a running event for people who were afraid to travel.

SEAN AS PADDY. You're not embarrassed of me then?

DINNY *gives him a look.*

DINNY. Keep an eye on Blake and Sean for us, Paddy, and make sure they don't torture anything.

SEAN AS PADDY. Righty ho!

SEAN *enters the right wardrobe. From inside an enormous scream of anguish:*

SEAN. FUCK!

BLAKE *and* DINNY *look towards the wardrobe and* DINNY *starts to laugh.*

DINNY. Good, Blake.

BLAKE. Thanks, Dad.

DINNY. Off ya go, son.

BLAKE *quickly puts on* EILEEN's *wig and walks into the bedroom and sees the coffin.*

BLAKE AS EILEEN. Oh my God what's this?!

SEAN *arrives fast as* PETER, *and, seeing the coffin:*

SEAN AS PETER. What the hell?!

BLAKE AS EILEEN. Who is that?

SEAN AS PETER. What's that smell of whiskey?

DINNY. It's my mother.

BLAKE AS EILEEN. What's your mother doing on my dining-room table, Denis?

DINNY. She's dead.

BLAKE AS EILEEN. You bring your dead mother on jobs with you?

SEAN AS PETER. You're using my sister's house for your dead mother's wake! You sneak!

BLAKE AS EILEEN. Oh, Denis . . .

DINNY (*snaps*). It's for Paddy! I know I shouldn't be here but I was doing it all for Paddy . . . because of his . . . condition.

BLAKE AS EILEEN. What condition, Denis?

A pause.

DINNY. Paddy's fallen on rough times, Eileen. Him and his wife Vera live destitute in a towerblock in London.

BLAKE AS EILEEN. So?

DINNY (*obviously thinking on his feet*). One day last year . . . Paddy, cold and shivering . . . walked down the Walworth Road and into a pet shop for some warmth. He was in there looking at the guppies in their tanks and talking to the budgies in their cages. The owner figured out that he was a retard so he let him at it.

BLAKE AS EILEEN (*lost*). Okay.

DINNY. Now Paddy was ravenous with the hunger. The last bit of solid to pass his lips was the nib of a bookie's pen and that was a whole week ago. There in the back of the pet shop, slunked in the corner . . . in an old crate . . . was a giant snake . . . called . . . the . . . (*Thinks hard.*) . . . Big . . . Langer Snake . . . eating a carrot. Well, Paddy, God bless him, didn't give it much thought, reached in and grabbed that Langer's dinner. When SNAP! Paddy was bitten and infected with a terrible snake venom.

BLAKE AS EILEEN. So is he dying?

DINNY. He will die, yeah. In the meantime his infected brain has started an unrelenting rot.

SEAN AS PETER. That would explain all his brain-surgeon nonsense.

DINNY. I took him here as a special treat, honest, Eileen. We were meant to bury Mammy today but Paddy wouldn't part with her. You arrived with your terrible news about your dead daddy and for some reason . . . Paddy's convinced that you're all brain surgeons intent on removing that snake venom from his miniscule brain.

Slight pause.

BLAKE AS EILEEN. I might have known that your reasons were for reasons of love. It's a wonderful thing to see such a bond between two family members.

SEAN AS PETER (*with true regret*). It's not always the case with us, is it, Eileen?

BLAKE AS EILEEN. With Denis's inspiration . . . I'm sure we can change, little brother.

A slight pause.

DINNY (*with relief and immense self-satisfaction*). Well, I don't know about you two but I could murder a drink!

DINNY *pops open a well-earned can of Harp.*

BLAKE AS JACK. I've been in the kitchen counting all the money. We're looking at fifty grand each, Peter!

SEAN AS PETER. I'm starting to feel uneasy about this.

BLAKE AS JACK. Uneasy?! Uneasy?! What do you mean?

SEAN AS PETER. Orchestrating Daddy's death was one thing but I can't stab my own sister in the back. It's her money too, Jack.

BLAKE AS JACK (*grabbing* SEAN AS PETER). Listen to me, you little shit! We had a deal. You've seen how she's treated me. Bullied in my own home so I have to spend my days sneaking around in the garden shed and drinking methylated spirits to keep myself sane!

SEAN AS PETER. Yes I . . .

BLAKE AS JACK. I deserve that money, you said so yourself. You back out on me now and I'll make shit of you, do you hear me! I'll have you, Peter. You and your sister, I swear it, man!

SEAN AS PETER. Oh Jack, come on!

BLAKE AS JACK *suddenly smacks* SEAN AS PETER *hard across the face. A little too hard.*

SEAN, *taken aback, dives at* BLAKE. *The two fall to the ground and start to fight each other.*

DINNY *nonchalantly walks past them and over to the kitchen and* HAYLEY.

He looks at her for some time.

DINNY. How's my chicken coming along?

A slight pause.

HAYLEY. It's heating in the oven.

DINNY. A lovely smell . . . roasting chicken.

HAYLEY *remains quiet.*

DINNY *drinks from his can of Harp.*

Thirsty work this. Drama piling on, isn't it?

HAYLEY. Yeah.

DINNY. Impressive work. Wonderful detail. (*A pause.*) Who d'you reckon has the best chance with the acting trophy today? Me is it? I'd be the best one, would I? Don't be shy!

HAYLEY. I suppose.

A pause.

DINNY. You're black. What are we going to do about that, Maureen?

DINNY *continues to drink his can of Harp and look at her.*

BLAKE *has* SEAN *on the ground and is strangling him.*

Realising what he's doing, BLAKE *stops. He remains sitting on* SEAN's *chest looking down on him.*

BLAKE (*quietly*). Were you talking to her about us? Are you trying to find ways to get us down to the streets? Send the little girl up and the door starts banging with more bodies wanting to get us. Are you turning your back on me, Sean?

DINNY *stands at the kitchen entrance looking in on the two of them.*

SEAN. I wouldn't do that. I couldn't be alone outside without you, Blake.

BLAKE. But you're wanting me to kill Dad, aren't you, Sean? We kill Dad, break the story, step outside like you've got it all planned . . . but then you walk away from me with her.

SEAN. With her?

BLAKE. You love her, tell me.

SEAN. Blake, we can both leave here. Me and you.

BLAKE. You can't deny you love her!

SEAN. You don't have to be scared of what's out there anymore.

BLAKE. WE BELONG IN HERE!

SEAN. Blake . . .

BLAKE *slaps him hard across the face.*

He climbs off SEAN *and stands over him.*

BLAKE. You break what I know and I give you my word, little brother, I'll have to kill you. (*Less sure.*) I can kill you straight.

SEAN. Then you'll live with what he lives with . . .

BLAKE. It's not true.

SEAN. I saw him, Blake. I saw the blood that day! It's all lies!

BLAKE. It was Mr Cotter and the poisoned chicken . . .

SEAN. Jesus, Blake . . .

BLAKE. No, Sean, no! No no no no!

SEAN. Blake!

BLAKE *covers his ears and enters the bedroom and lies on the bed with his head beneath the pillow.*

SEAN *remains lying on the floor. He then notices* DINNY *standing looking down at him. He must have heard what he just said.*

DINNY. All a little bit fucked today, isn't it, Sean?

SEAN. Yes, Dad.

DINNY. Come here to me so.

> DINNY *walks back inside the kitchen.*
>
> SEAN *gets up and walks inside too.*
>
> HAYLEY *stands at the cooker and* DINNY *sits at the table.* SEAN *stands by the entrance.*
>
> *A pause.*

Tell me what you remember the day I left Cork, Sean.

SEAN. Why?

DINNY. Well, is it the same as the way we tell it?

> *A pause.*

SEAN. No.

> *A pause.*

DINNY. No? (*He's angry but keeps calm. A pause.*) Let me hear it so I can see where I stand with ya. You're playing in Mrs Cotter's back garden.

SEAN (*a pause*). No, Dad. We're playing in our back garden me and Blake. Granny's coffin's open in the front room and the room smells of dust so you send us out into the fresh air. We're lying on the grass and we're talking about what we'll be when we're all grown up. Blake full of talk about being an astronaut. He's read a book on it and he knows some big words to do with space. He says he'd feel safe up there. He said if he got nervous he'd hide the Earth behind his thumb. He talked about a parade in Dublin when the space men got back from space. How there'd have to be a special parade for him in Cork and everyone would come out and cheer him on and slag off the Dubs. We're just sitting on the grass chatting like that. (*A pause.*) I say I want to be a bus driver because I like buses and Blake thinks that it's a great job. Just like driving a rocket 'cept your orbit's the Grand Parade and Mac Curtain Street. (*A pause.*) There's shouting from inside the house. You and Uncle Paddy screaming at

58

each other. Fighting over Granny's money even before she's stuck in the ground. Aunty Vera crying her cries real high like a baby crying. Your voice so much bigger than Uncle Paddy and him saying, 'No, Dinny, no please, Dinny!' (*Slight pause*.) And then we hear Mammy screaming, Dad. We're both up fast and running through our back door and into our kitchen and the smell of the roast chicken. Her screaming coming from the sitting room and Blake won't go inside 'cause he's frightened of what he might see. But I do. I do go inside. And Mammy grabs me and spins me around fast so I can't see . . . but I see Uncle Paddy and Aunty Vera on the ground and I see you standing in the corner with blood all over your hands. There's blood on your hands and a kitchen knife, I'm sure of it. (*A pause*.) Mam's terrible screaming. And you're standing at the door and I can see that you're trying to make up your mind whether to stay or to run. And Mammy kisses you and says, 'Leave, now', and sets you free. You just step out to the outside and begin your run.

A long pause.

DINNY. Why did your mammy send you two little boys right after me if I did a bad thing?

SEAN. Because she still loved you. Because what we had used to be so good in Ireland. Maybe she could forgive you. (*Slight pause*.) Dad, I don't know why she sent us.

A pause.

Momentarily, DINNY *is affected by what* SEAN *says.*

DINNY. I'm keeping you and Blake safe.

SEAN. I know you think that.

DINNY (*aggravated now*). FUCK!!

HAYLEY *flinches.*

(*Quickly.*) So what did you two talk about?

DINNY *turns* HAYLEY *around to face him.*

You talked this morning in Tesco, didn't you? Talkin' about what we get up to in here, Sean?

SEAN. No, Dad.

DINNY places SEAN opposite HAYLEY.

DINNY. Don't be lying to me and tell me what was said. Show me exactly how it was. The same words. Play it. (*To* HAYLEY.) Sit down!

He sits HAYLEY down by the table.

(*To* SEAN.) You walk up to her and you say:

HAYLEY. All right?

DINNY. And you say what then?

SEAN. Hello.

DINNY. Do the shopping, come on, come on!

HAYLEY mimes scanning SEAN's shopping.

DINNY mimes packing the shopping into a plastic bag.

(*To* HAYLEY.) And you say?

HAYLEY. Same shopping as usual? (*Breaks.*) Look, please let me leave!

DINNY (*snaps*). Again again!

HAYLEY. Same shopping as usual?

SEAN. And I laugh a little for no good reason. (*Slight pause. To* HAYLEY.) I'm so sorry.

HAYLEY breaks down again.

DINNY shakes her to talk. A pause as she controls herself.

HAYLEY. Are you doing anything at the weekend? It's just I might go down to Brighton Beach, have you ever been there?

SEAN. No.

HAYLEY. It's nice. Maybe you'd like to go there with me sometime.

BLAKE appears out of the bedroom and stands listening to SEAN and HAYLEY talking in the kitchen.

SEAN. And I can't say anything as I pack the shopping away. (*Slight pause.*) But I'm thinking of whether I could ever risk my life with somebody else. If there would ever come a time when someone would promise me a new start. I'm thinking about us walking on a beach by the sea and I'm wondering if you'd stay with me if I got outside, Hayley. But you can't see me thinking about all of that. And I want to say, 'I'd really like to go there one day.'

HAYLEY *almost smiles.*

HAYLEY. Then I would say, 'Let's go, Sean. Let's leave now.'

A slight pause.

SEAN (*quietly*). You would?

BLAKE *hits the play button on the tape recorder and 'A Nation Once Again' blares loudly out.*

He starts to thrash the flat.

DINNY *goes to the sitting room to see him. He starts to laugh.*

DINNY. Good man, Blake! That a boy! Go on now! Go on, Blake!

Everything's unravelling.

SEAN *looks very worried. Suddenly he notices* HAYLEY's *holding his hand.*

She gestures that her phone is in her bag in the sitting room and that SEAN *should get it.*

DINNY *turns and grabs* SEAN *and throws him out into the sitting room.*

BLAKE *continues demolishing the flat as* SEAN *watches him.*

DINNY *turns off the music.*

(*Snaps.*) Enough, Blake!

BLAKE *stops. He stares at* SEAN, *strikes him hard across the face.*

SEAN *hits the ground*.

BLAKE AS JACK (*announcing*). Anyone care where I am . . . I'm in the garden shed!

BLAKE AS JACK *walks quickly away and enters a wardrobe and closes the door*.

DINNY (*threatening* SEAN). You back down, do you hear me?

BLAKE *re-enters fast as* VERA *and heads for* SEAN AS PETER *as he gets up*.

BLAKE AS VERA. Did Jack hurt you, Peter love? You had an argument, did ya?! I know what you science types are like. Fierce competitive. Good Christ, I like your style! You make my Paddy look like another species.

SEAN AS PETER (*dazed*). I can't understand what you're doing with Paddy, Vera. Having loyalty to a man with his condition.

BLAKE AS VERA. Sure Paddy's hole is only a part of his problem.

SEAN AS PETER. What a beautiful lady you are.

BLAKE AS VERA. At last someone to scoop me up in their arms and ride me horse back down Walworth Road to sunnier and better climes!

SEAN *returns to the wardrobe*.

DINNY (*walking into the bedroom, mid-conversation*). I hear what you're saying, Eileen, but I've only got so much love to spread about, darling.

BLAKE AS EILEEN. But that wife of yours!

DINNY. Boring she might be. The personality of a dead fish, she most certainly has, but what Maureen can do in the kitchen. Like a wizard in there.

BLAKE AS EILEEN. But in the bedroom, Denis? How is she in the bedroom.

DINNY. She can give as good as she gets.

BLAKE AS EILEEN. You see that's the sort of talk I like to hear from a real man!

DINNY. Oh now, Eileen, please! There's one thing cheating on my unsuspecting and stupid wife and another thing entirely bringing disgrace on my dear mother as she lies in her eternal sleep.

SEAN *opens the wardrobe door to sneak out into the room and get* HAYLEY*'s bag.*

BLAKE AS EILEEN. Such a strange expression she has on her face, Denis.

BLAKE AS EILEEN *looks in the coffin,*

DINNY. She has. As if she's bitten into a lemon.

BLAKE AS EILEEN. Not the sort of face you want to wear in eternal life.

DINNY. That's true . . . but the poor love didn't have a choice. Reconstructed her head and face was . . . Hang on a sec . . .

SEAN *is back in the wardrobe fast as* DINNY *walks from the bedroom through the sitting room and into the kitchen.*

(*Glancing at* HAYLEY.) Carry on, carry on!

He takes up a washing-up-liquid bottle and fills it with water.

He returns to the bedroom with the bottle and takes up his position.

Again, Blake.

BLAKE AS EILEEN. Such a strange expression she has on her face, Denis.

DINNY. She has. As if she's bitten into a lemon, Eileen.

BLAKE AS EILEEN. Not the sort of face you want to wear in eternal life.

DINNY. That's true . . . but the poor love didn't have a choice. Reconstructed her head and face was but . . .

He squirts some water from the bottle into his eyes to effect tears.

(*Getting emotional.*) . . . but not by the highly qualified surgeon as we wished, Eileen. It was a price we couldn't afford.

BLAKE AS EILEEN. Whose hands done the deed so, Denis?

DINNY. The hands and the deed were mine, Eileen. Though to be honest I can't remember much about it. It wouldn't be every day that a son is called upon to stitch up his dead mother's pulverised face, so I had a few drinks to lessen the shock. The only previous stitching experience I had was a scarf I knitted when I was a schoolboy.

BLAKE AS EILEEN. Is that what accounts for the length of her chin?

DINNY. It is.

BLAKE AS EILEEN. And the little bobbles at the end?

DINNY. I was getting carried away at that point.

DINNY *looks at the bottle.*

Genius! Fucking genius, boy!

DINNY *runs from the bedroom and into the sitting room. He grabs the acting trophy from its shelf and kisses it.*

Is there anyone better?! Might I ever be challenged, tell me!?

SEAN AS PADDY *appears, thundering out of the wardrobe. His performance seemingly back on track.*

SEAN AS PADDY. It's Mrs Cotter's house!?! Say it isn't so, Dinny. Say it isn't so! Lying to me like that. You of the red wine and green Pringles!

DINNY. Ah bollix!

SEAN AS PADDY. That Mr Cotter told me whose house it is before he legged it into that garden shed. You know of the poverty . . .

DINNY. ' . . . before he legged it into that garden shed and into that yellow frock.' Fuck it, Sean, come on, COME ON,

BOY! Mr Cotter, yellow frock, poison in the bucket, making the blue sauce for the cooked chicken! Details, details!

SEAN. I remember, Dad!

DINNY. Remember nothing! Say the line!

SEAN AS PADDY. That Mr Cotter told me whose house it is before he legged it into that garden shed and into that yellow frock! You know of the terrible poverty me and Vera are under. You whisk us up here with your airs and graces, spin out Mammy's will and fob me off with a monthly allowance and three cans of Harp. Shame on you! Shame on you, Dinny!

When DINNY *turns away,* SEAN *grabs* HAYLEY*'s bag from off the floor and hides it behind his back.*

DINNY. He's losing it big time, Eileen.

SEAN AS PADDY. Losing nothing. Gaining is what I'm doing. Gaining my rightful half to Mammy's estate.

BLAKE AS VERA. You using a time of grief to rob a man of his rightful inheritance!

SEAN AS PADDY. Go on, Vera! Go on!!

BLAKE AS VERA. Any man with average intelligence would have copped onto you a long time ago, Dinny. But you taking advantage of Paddy's tiny minuscule brain. A man who thought that cats laid eggs. That Walt Disney discovered America . . .

SEAN AS PADDY. All right, Vera . . .

BLAKE AS VERA. . . . . and that fish actually had fingers. Well, shame on you for this, Dinny!

DINNY (*snaps*). Yerrah, shut up out of that with your 'shame'!

DINNY *crashes into the kitchen as does* BLAKE, *who's now playing* MAUREEN.

HAYLEY*'s startled.*

Fuck it, Maureen we're fucked!

BLAKE AS MAUREEN. What, love?

DINNY. Paddy and Vera knows whose house it is, pet. Time to pack up Mammy and get the hell out of here.

BLAKE AS MAUREEN. Smashed are we?

DINNY. Dead in the water, love. Might get a few bob for Mammy's coffin, otherwise we're smashed.

BLAKE AS MAUREEN. Take a look in there and see if it doesn't cheer you up.

DINNY *looks and holds up some Monopoly money.*

DINNY. Holy be jaynee! What's this!?

BLAKE AS MAUREEN. Only them two other men know of it. It's half Mrs Cotter's but she doesn't have a clue, Dinny. If there was any way we could swindle the money out of her.

DINNY. Swindle this money out of Mrs Cotter, but how??!

DINNY *and* BLAKE *walk fast out of the kitchen and through the sitting room.*

A word in your ear, Eileen.

SEAN *throws the bag in to* HAYLEY.

BLAKE AS EILEEN. Why's it you told your brother Paddy that this was your house, Denis?

In her hand, HAYLEY*'s mobile phone suddenly plays the Crazy Frog version of Destiny Child's 'I'm a Survivor'.*

HAYLEY. Shit shit!

DINNY. What the fuck is that?!

SEAN *grabs* EILEEN*'s wig off* BLAKE *and continues speaking so as to mask the phone noise.*

SEAN AS EILEEN. Why's it you told your brother Paddy this was your house, Denis?

DINNY (*distracted*). 'Cause it's a deep bond between me and you, Eileen. For bonded through grief and tragedy we are.

DINNY *looking for the source of the noise.*

SEAN AS EILEEN. Tragedy, Denis? *Cein fath?*

BLAKE *is confused as he takes the wig back from* SEAN.

DINNY. That horse which killed your dear daddy as he sped through that field in his speedboat . . . that very same horse crushed my mammy as she picked gooseberries on a quiet country road.

The ring tone stops.

BLAKE AS EILEEN. The very same horse that my Dad ploughed into?

DINNY. That's the one.

BLAKE AS EILEEN. She was killed by my father so?

DINNY. And here we are left picking up the pieces, Eileen.

SEAN AS EILEEN. For her to be slain by my own father. If there was any way I could financially compensate you for this great tragedy. Anything . . . Anything at all . . .

BLAKE *suddenly realises something is up.*

HAYLEY *hides beneath the kitchen table.*

HAYLEY (*talking into the phone*). Mum, it's me! I'm in a flat on the Walworth Road . . . Will you stop talking and listen to me!

BLAKE *grabs* HAYLEY *from beneath the table. She screams and drops the phone.*

DINNY *is furious that the Farce has broken down once again.*

DINNY (*shouts*). Ah for fuck's sake!

BLAKE *drags* HAYLEY *screaming across the sitting room, picks up her coat and gets her inside the bedroom.*

DINNY *holds* SEAN *back as he tries to stop* BLAKE. *He fires him against the wardrobe.*

SEAN *collapses on the ground.*

DINNY *enters the kitchen and sees the phone on the ground.*

BLAKE *has thrown* HAYLEY *on the bed and is tying her arms behind her back. He then begins to gag her to stop her screaming.*

DINNY *picks up the phone and is amazed by it. He listens to the frantic voice on the other end.*

Hello? Am I holding a phone?

He opens the oven door and throws the phone inside and slams the door shut.

He takes the large kitchen knife from the table and leaves the kitchen. He grabs SEAN *by the hair and drags him to the armchair, making him sit.*

Standing behind him he holds the knife hard against SEAN*'s throat.*

BLAKE *steps back from* HAYLEY *who lies face down on the bed, her arms bound. He then puts on her coat.*

SEAN. I won't go on.

DINNY. Of course you will.

SEAN. I can't, Dad.

DINNY. Sean . . .

SEAN. Dad, please, I can't do it anymore.

DINNY *presses the knife in harder into* SEAN*'s throat.*

BLAKE *goes to the bedroom door and looks into the sitting room at the two of them.*

DINNY. Mammy making the macaroni cheese on a Tuesday, Sean. The two washed boys wrapped up in their dressing gowns on Saturday nights. Sunday morning and the four of us watching the Walton family on the telly with our dinner cooking in the kitchen. Friday night and in the pub for a feed of pints but I'm back home to kiss you little boys to beddy-byes just like Daddy Walton would. (*Slight pause.*) The family routine keeping things safe, Sean. I lived like that in Cork. I was a good man. (*A long pause.*) You looking

in at Paddy and Vera dead on the floor like you said. My
hand shaking. Real blood on the carpet. Me telling your
mam, 'I'm off to London to make my fortune, Maureen. I'll
send for you, Maureen, and we will be happy.' Her little
kiss to me and telling me, 'Leave now.' I'm about to leave
but I see you looking at me. Looking for answers, aren't ya?
I turn and go. I go. In London and I'm standing in the
roundabout in Elephant and Castle with all its noise and
people, fuck it. 'Run, Dinny boy. Run.' Start running and
get inside to Paddy's flat. These pictures of Paddy and Vera
on the walls looking down at me, you see them? Asking me
questions I can't answer, Sean. With every breath more
scared of them. (*Slight pause.*) There's a knock on the door
and it's you two boys standing there off the bus from Cork
City, by jaynee. Sent by Mammy to ask me back to Cork,
aren't ya. My little boys back to me. 'Hello little boys.
Come on in, boys.' I wrap you up in a towel and hold ya.
'All right boys! Sure it's Daddy here, look. Ohh my little
John Boy and Jim Bob! It's lovely to see ya again, boys!'
To calm you down, Sean, I start to tell you the story of me
and Paddy on Robert's Cove beach. Me with Daddy's towel
wrapping Paddy up and keeping him safe. For days I play
that story over and over for you and Blakey and it brings us
some calm and peace of mind. The telling of the story . . . it
helps me, Sean. (*A pause.*) 'Daddy?' 'Yes, Seanie?' 'What
happened back home in Cork, Daddy?' (*A pause.*) I start to
tell a new story. (*Almost breaks.*) My head, Sean.

DINNY *clutches at his head in real pain.*

SEAN *just looks at him.*

The pain slowly goes. He lowers his hands from his head.

A pause.

DINNY *looks right through him.*

We're making a routine that keeps our family safe. Isn't that
what we've done here?

A slight pause.

SEAN. But none of these words are true.

A pause.

DINNY. It's my truth, nothing else matters. (*A pause.*) You can never leave here without poor Blake, can you, Sean?

SEAN. No, Dad.

DINNY. 'No, Dad.' To step outside and just little you all alone out there in the world, imagine that?

SEAN*'s eyes fill with tears.*

It could never happen, Sean, answer me.

SEAN. I couldn't be alone outside, Dad.

DINNY. No need, Seanie boy, no need at all.

SEAN *crying a little and* DINNY *embraces him.*

A pause.

You'll never tell Blake what you seen that last day, Sean?

SEAN. I wouldn't do that to him.

DINNY. A simple boy best kept in the dark, isn't he?

SEAN. It's a better place to be.

A pause.

DINNY. To kill me would only turn you into your dad. Isn't that what you're thinking, Sean? Answer me, boy.

A long pause.

So you're not going to kill me then?

A pause.

Hah?

SEAN *doesn't answer.*

Hearing enough, BLAKE *returns to* HAYLEY *and starts to untie her.*

It would never happen on *The Waltons.* Can't imagine John Boy or Jim Bob raising a nasty hand to Daddy Walton, can ya? Never in a million years, despite all those wood-carving tools hanging about their house, would you see such a thing on Walton Mountain, Sean.

The embrace breaks and DINNY *looks at* SEAN.

Get back to my story. Get ready for the big finish, Sean.
Soon Paddy's hole will strike and off to meet the good
Lord, God bless him. Play it big and clear for me, won't ya?

SEAN. I will, Dad.

DINNY. Acting trophy could be yours, Sean. I'm rooting for
you, boy.

A pause.

SEAN. Will you let her go when we finish today?

DINNY. I will let her go if you're a good boy to me.

SEAN. All right, Dad.

HAYLEY *sits on the bed with* BLAKE *standing in her coat
looking down at her.*

HAYLEY. Do you want to be me?

BLAKE. No.

BLAKE *takes off her coat and hands it to her.*

HAYLEY. How long have you been doing this? (*Slight pause.*)
Can't you leave?

BLAKE *doesn't answer. A pause.*

BLAKE. If Sean can go, you'll be with him? You won't leave
Sean alone outside, promise me.

A slight pause.

HAYLEY. I'll stay with him.

BLAKE. Cross your heart and hope to die.

A slight pause.

HAYLEY. Cross my heart and hope to die.

A pause.

BLAKE. I can finish it so.

For the final time DINNY *plays 'A Nation Once Again' on
the tape recorder.*

BLAKE *and* SEAN *take up their positions.* BLAKE *goes to the kitchen and stands looking into the coffin as* EILEEN *and* SEAN *stands where* SEAN AS PADDY *was standing previously.*

DINNY *looks at* HAYLEY *as she makes her way back over to the kitchen. She drops her coat by the door.*

She looks towards SEAN *and him at her. But she knows she's by herself now. She enters the kitchen and finishes preparing the lunch.*

Everything in its proper place and DINNY *turns off the tape recorder and enters the kitchen fast.*

DINNY. So what exactly are you saying about compensation, Eileen, for my mother's death at the hands of your daddy's speedboat. We can go halves, is it?

BLAKE AS EILEEN. This terrific money could all be yours, Denis. Just say the word and it could be you and me . . .

BLAKE AS MAUREEN (*snaps*). Dinny!

DINNY *and* BLAKE AS EILEEN (*startled*). Ahhh!

DINNY. Yerrah for fuck sake, Maureen, do you have to creep around like that!?

BLAKE AS MAUREEN. It's the money you're after and not that slapper, right? (*Pleading.*) You wouldn't leave me for Eileen, Dinny?

DINNY (*whispering*). Course I wouldn't, sweetheart. You'll have plenty of dinner days ahead of ya. Now shut up and cook!

DINNY *exits the kitchen.* SEAN AS PADDY *turns away from him and enters the bedroom.*

SEAN AS PADDY. There he is, the man who tried to rob me blind.

BLAKE *enters the stage right wardrobe.*

Stay away from me now for I have no family but for Mammy here.

DINNY. She's dead, Paddy. She's dead.

SEAN AS PADDY. I'm aware she's dead, Dinny. Well aware of that fact. You've tricked me for the last time, boy! A brother of mine you are no longer.

BLAKE *re-enters as* JACK *wearing a yellow frock. He holds a bucket with a yellow poison symbol painted on it. He enters the kitchen and starts to boil up some milk in a pan, and empties some of the blue contents of the bucket into it.* HAYLEY *looks on.*

DINNY. Seeing our dead mammy on that country road it threw me into a terrible despair. Lies I started to spin. Lies against the only brother I ever had. Sure I couldn't carry on with you cut out from my life, Paddy.

SEAN AS PADDY. You have done for ten years.

DINNY. That's right, you're right. But this afternoon has set me straight, Paddy. The bond is being built, I swear it.

SEAN AS PADDY. It is?

DINNY. You're my brother, Paddy, and for the life of me I don't know why I like ya. A sad day today with our mammy stuck in that box but a happy day for our reunion. So what say you of a reconciliation, oh little brother of mine? (*He holds out a can of beer.*)

SEAN AS PADDY *grabs it and knocks it back fast.*

SEAN *exits the bedroom and meets* BLAKE *who exits the kitchen where he's left* HAYLEY *stirring the pan of milk.*

BLAKE AS VERA. Mr Cotter's in the kitchen, Peter, with a bucket of poison! A yellow frock he has on! I caught Paddy wearing a pair of my knickers once. Standing on a chair and hanging a light bulb he was. It was like watching *The Dam Busters*. Sooner or later the walls of them knickers were bound to . . .

SEAN AS PETER. You know it's difficult for me to be hearing that, Vera sweetheart.

BLAKE AS VERA. You can imagine what it was like seeing it.

SEAN AS PETER. So Jack must be planning to poison me and my sister Eileen so the money can all be his. Well, we'll see about that!

BLAKE *enters the kitchen as* JACK.

BLAKE AS JACK. Just pour it over the chicken like I said, Maureen! I'm not standing here arguing with you about savoury sauces when there's a coffin of money that needs liberating.

During the following, SEAN *lights a fire lighter and throws it into the right wardrobe.*

DINNY (*entering kitchen*). Ah Mr Cotter!

BLAKE AS JACK. Suppose you're wondering what I'm doing wearing this yellow frock?

DINNY. Looks like you're making a sauce for the chicken, Jack.

BLAKE AS JACK. True but the bigger picture will speak of my new-found freedom, Denis.

DINNY. A fight worth fighting for if you don't mind me saying so, Jackie.

DINNY *pats him on the backside.*

BLAKE AS JACK. Exactly the sort of confidence boost that's needed before facing the dragon-lady herself!

BLAKE *exits the kitchen.*

Afternoon, Eileen!

BLAKE AS EILEEN (*screeches*). Oh my sweet Jesus!

Suddenly BLAKE *covers* SEAN*'s mouth with his hand.*

BLAKE. I'm ready to kill her if that's what it takes.

SEAN*, freaked, slaps his hand away.*

SEAN. No, Blake!

BLAKE. Just like Dad, Sean!

DINNY (*to* HAYLEY). What the hell's he up to, Maureen?

Slight pause.

HAYLEY. What?

BLAKE *and* SEAN *freeze and look through the open kitchen door.*

DINNY (*smiling*). So you got the lunch made the way I told ya, Maureen?

HAYLEY. Yeah.

DINNY. 'Yes, Dinny.'

HAYLEY. Yes, Dinny.

DINNY. Good girl. Little pink wafers too?

HAYLEY. I broke them up and made them into a heart shape like you said.

He smiles back to BLAKE *and* SEAN.

DINNY. Good work, Maureen. And what's that weird smell, love?

HAYLEY. Just coloured milk, I think.

DINNY *takes* MAUREEN*'s wig off* BLAKE*'s head and puts it on* HAYLEY.

BLAKE *gets the kitchen knife from the coffee table.* SEAN *tries to wrestle it off him.*

DINNY. What's that weird smell, love? (*Instructing* HAYLEY *in her line.*) 'You've got to stay away from the chicken, Dinny.'

HAYLEY (*crying, slowly*). You've got to stay away from the chicken, Dinny.

DINNY. Oh Jesus, love, I can't. Sure amn't I famished for chicken. A day of deceit and lies and I'm fit to eat a horse, by jaynee. (*Instructing her.*) 'Mr Cotter's trying to poison his wife and Peter with the chicken.'

BLAKE *walks fast into the wardrobe.*

SEAN *relieved that he's gone but still freaked out.*

HAYLEY. Mr Cotter's trying to poison his wife and Peter with the chicken.

DINNY. Poison, Maureen?

HAYLEY (*offering a new line*). Well, I saw Mr Cotter with a bucket of poison. He got me to mix it with the milk to pour it over the chicken.

DINNY (*impressed*). So he wants you to put the poisoned sauce on the chicken to kill Peter and Eileen and trick them by saying that it is in fact your special sauce, Maureen?

HAYLEY. I suppose.

DINNY (*explaining*). See, that way Peter and Vera will take the poisoned chicken thinking that it's just one of Maureen's savoury sensations. Do your new line again.

HAYLEY. I saw Mr Cotter with a bucket of poison. He got me to mix it with the milk to pour it over the chicken.

DINNY. Well, far be it for me to stand in his way. Pour away, Maureen!

DINNY *makes* HAYLEY *pour the sky-blue sauce over the pieces of chicken.* DINNY *gives* SEAN *the 'thumbs up'.*

(*To* HAYLEY.) Fair dues. You're keeping up so far.

BLAKE *is heard screaming from the smoking wardrobe.*

By jaynee what's this?!

DINNY *races into the sitting room.*

BLAKE, *as his seven-year-old self, appears out of the wardrobe carrying a smouldering stuffed dog with a tent pole up its backside.* SEAN *quickly joins him.*

Speak up and don't be hiding nothing from your daddy.

BLAKE. Minding our own business we were.

SEAN. Big barks and Bouncer hops over the fence like a wild horse.

BLAKE. Wild he is from the pain of the tent pole still up his arse, Dad.

SEAN. It didn't seem right that one of God's animals could be in such torture so Blake made chase.

BLAKE. He took some chasing though. Through the estate and back again.

SEAN. Cornered back in the garden with the pole like a deadly weapon in Bouncer's backside. Into the garden shed he runs. We follow him inside the shed, Dad, and there he lies almost dead, the poor thing.

BLAKE. Pull with all my might and that pole wouldn't budge an inch.

SEAN. Lubrication it needed. Some figure of liquid in a bottle on a shelf I applied to the doggy.

BLAKE. Still not a budge no matter how hard I pulled.

SEAN. He's frozen with the soaking now and Blake tells me to stick his shaking battered body next to the two-bar heater. When BANG!!

BLAKE. He's lit up like a firework all of a sudden! Sure when did Sean ever see methylated spirits, Dad?

SEAN. And when did I hear such screaming from one animal. Flames firing him back on his feet and Bouncer's away like a bat out of hell.

BLAKE. Thankfully the sorry sight came to a stop shortly afterwards.

DINNY. Heart attack, was it?

SEAN. Blake struck him clean with the shovel, Dad.

BLAKE. In fairness he took a few strikes. He was a great little fighter.

DINNY. Good lads.

BLAKE *and* SEAN *exit with the smouldering stuffed dog through the right wardrobe.*

A pause.

(*To* HAYLEY.) You didn't see that coming.

HAYLEY. No.

DINNY. Tying up loose ends, teasing out the big finish. (*Shouting*.) Move it, lads! Move it!

SEAN and BLAKE re-enter immediately. BLAKE still holds the kitchen knife in his hand and SEAN sees this.

SEAN. Fuck it, he's allowing her to leave, Blake! We can get back to normal! Tell him, Dad!

DINNY (*announcing big*). Maureen, the chicken, love.

SEAN tries to take the knife off BLAKE.

SEAN. Please, Blake, no!!

DINNY (*shouts*). Maureen, move it!

HAYLEY enters still wearing MAUREEN's wig and carrying the chicken on a tray.

She looks at SEAN but he looks helpless.

Hang on a sec!

DINNY takes his moisturiser and whitens HAYLEY's face.

That's more like it. Lovely, Maureen! (*Snaps*.) Kitchen, Sean! Sean as Peter, come on, come on! Poison the lager, sneaky Pete, give it to Jack, do it, do it!

SEAN AS PETER goes to the kitchen and sees the bucket of 'poison'. He empties some of its contents into a can of beer. He leans over against the sideboard and holds his head momentarily.

You like the look of your Mammy, Blake.

BLAKE. Yes, Dad. (*Slight pause*.) Scream!

BLAKE suddenly does a movement where he turns quickly towards the wardrobe and holds his arms above his head. He drops his arms and turns back to the kitchen entrance.

Scream!

Again he does the movement. Again he turns back. He's practising something.

Scream!

Again the movement. DINNY looks on bemused.

DINNY. Feck it, you're some tulip. (*With energy.*) Chicken everyone?!

BLAKE *takes the tray from HAYLEY and indicates for her to return to the kitchen.*

SEAN (*snaps*). Fuck it!

SEAN *quickly opens up a drawer in the kitchen and takes out a knife. He faces the kitchen entrance. He then puts the knife in the pocket of his jacket.*

SEAN AS PETER *appears through the other door, holding the can of 'poisoned' lager as HAYLEY enters the kitchen.*

BLAKE AS JACK *snatches the can of beer off SEAN AS PETER.*

BLAKE AS JACK. Cheers, Peter.

SEAN AS PETER. Be my guest.

BLAKE AS VERA (*whispering*). Is that lager poisoned then, Peter?

SEAN AS PETER. The scene's set and soon on a beach we'll lie, Vera.

BLAKE AS JACK. Chicken, Dinny?

DINNY. No chicken for me, Jackie, today's grief has tied my stomach into a tight knot smaller than a gnat's arse.

SEAN AS PADDY. Nor me, Jack. My stomach couldn't handle solids. 'Less you can liquidise that chicken into a savoury shake, it's useless to me.

BLAKE AS JACK. Some of Maureen's special sauce then, Paddy?

SEAN AS PADDY (*eyeing up his can of beer*). There's only one sauce you're holding that interests me.

BLAKE AS JACK *holds the beer out to SEAN AS PADDY but, as is his physical catchphrase, pulls it away at the last moment and knocks it back fast.*

Sacriligious, boy. Sacriligious.

BLAKE AS JACK. And finally you Eileen, my wife. A little bit of food needed after the shock of seeing your husband looking so good in a frock?

BLAKE AS EILEEN. It's a whole chicken that's needed, Jack.

BLAKE AS EILEEN wolfs down a half of chicken.

BLAKE AS JACK. Eat away, Eileen! Eat away!

BLAKE AS JACK laughs but suddenly a jolt of pain in his stomach as the poison kicks in. He stares at the can he just drank from.

(*Groaning.*) I'll be feeling this in the morning.

BLAKE AS JACK collapses and dies.

SEAN AS PETER. Let's eat to our bright future so, Vera.

BLAKE AS VERA is up fast.

BLAKE AS VERA. Jack dead, then?

SEAN AS PETER. Never again to don the nylons, Vera.

BLAKE AS VERA. Feed us a leg off that chicken so and let us toast our new-found love, Peter!

A chicken leg each and they feed each other.

SEAN AS PADDY (*shocked*). What's this, Vera!?

Suddenly he holds his heart in pain.

Oh good God no. Not now! Not here!

DINNY. Paddy? Paddy, what is it, little brother?!

SEAN AS PADDY. The wife's turned, Dinny. Turned from me with that knobber Peter and in doing so has fired my fragile hole.

SEAN AS PADDY drops to his knees.

It's smaller I'm getting! Smaller!

DINNY. You're on your knees, Paddy.

SEAN AS PADDY. So I am! But sure isn't every Irishman! (*Screams.*) ERIN GO BRAGH!

SEAN AS PADDY *falls over on the floor and dies*.

BLAKE AS VERA. With Paddy the husband gone I'm all yours, Peter love!

BLAKE AS VERA *holds his stomach in pain*.

Oh sweet Jesus! What poisoned trickery is this?

SEAN AS PETER (*holding his stomach in pain*). I fear we've come undone, Vera. Our budding love affair cut short and a shame I'll never get to see you in the nip!

BLAKE AS VERA. Likewise, Peter! It would have been nice to wake up to a virile man as opposed to my Paddy who God bless him was hung like a hamster.

They both drop to their knees and hold hands.

They collapse dead.

BLAKE *gets up and puts on* EILEEN*'s wig*.

DINNY *looks at* BLAKE AS EILEEN.

DINNY. Eileen, love, don't tell me you had a piece of that poisoned chicken, did ya?

BLAKE AS EILEEN. Never a woman to pass up free grub, Dinny. And never a better man has profited from death. (*Holding his stomach and dropping to his knees*.) The money is all yours! Oh the pain, Dinny, the pain. For me to be cut down in my prime. A woman to be robbed of what the world has to offer! Like a banker without a bank, a journalist without a journal, a painter without paint . . .

DINNY. All right, Blake!

BLAKE AS EILEEN. Cheerio, oh chosen one.

BLAKE AS EILEEN *dies*.

A pause.

DINNY *rushes into the kitchen all excited and starts filling his pockets with Monopoly money*.

SEAN *and* BLAKE *get to their feet and stand opposite each other as they hold their knives in their hands*.

The two brothers stare at each other as DINNY *continues inside the kitchen.*

BLAKE. I'm ready to kill her.

SEAN. I won't let you do it, Blake.

BLAKE. A coward like you?!

DINNY (*shouts inside*). Wardrobe, Sean! Move it! SEAN!

BLAKE *grabs* SEAN *and throws him into the wardrobe. He puts a large latch on it to lock* SEAN *inside.*

SEAN (*from inside*). NO!

DINNY (*triumphant*). Well, Maureen, the day of the dead it most certainly is! But even in violent death some glimmer of hope must be sought. Sure aren't people great all the same. A kick in the face and they'll come up smiling. Backs to the wall and it's best foot forward.

DINNY *leaves the kitchen for the sitting room.* HAYLEY *stands at the kitchen door looking at him.*

So away to London I am. Away to treble my new-found wealth and build for us a castle to overlook the English scum. There we'll sit, Maureen, lording over the lot of them, a bit of Cork up there in the sky. It's soon I'll call for you, Maureen. (*Rubbing moisturiser into his face.*) 'Tween now and then keep youthful, love, and I too won't change a jot. Lines won't grow on this face and hair still as thick as a brush, by Christ.

BLAKE AS MAUREEN (*firm*). Yes, Dinny. I'll wait home in Cork for you.

DINNY *throws an arm around* BLAKE *and gives him a little hug. The knife held tight in* BLAKE*'s hand about to strike.*

DINNY. A day of twists and turns and ducks and dives and terrible shocks. A story to be retold, no doubt, and cast in lore. For what are we, Maureen, if we're not our stories?

BLAKE. We're the lost and the lonely.

DINNY. Away to London! Gather around, my little boys!

Come and kiss your daddy a final farewell!

BLAKE *fires the knife into* DINNY*'s back.*

DINNY *gasps.* BLAKE *pulls out the knife, turns* DINNY *towards him quickly and stabs him in the stomach hard.*

(In pain he continues.) Away . . . away . . .

BLAKE *(quietly he prompts him).* 'Away but soon . . .'

DINNY. Away but soon . . . Trophy, Blake. Trophy.

BLAKE *hands him his acting trophy.*

BLAKE. 'Away but soon and I'll return to Cork, Maureen.' Say it, Dad.

DINNY *watches the blood pour from his stomach.*

DINNY. Fuck it, that's some acting. Real blood. The blood and bandage, Blake, hah? *(Slight pause.)* Away but soon and I'll return to Cork, Maureen.

DINNY *kisses his trophy.*

HAYLEY *stands in the kitchen entrance petrified.*

BLAKE *(to* HAYLEY*).* Latch.

HAYLEY *goes to the wardrobe and holds the latch. She looks at* BLAKE.

(Calmly to HAYLEY*.)* Scream.

HAYLEY *screams and opens the latch fast.*

BLAKE *suddenly does the movement where he turns quickly towards the wardrobe and holds his arms above his head.*

SEAN *runs from the wardrobe and drives his knife into* BLAKE*'s stomach.*

DINNY *slumps to the ground dead.*

BLAKE *slumps against* SEAN.

Only now does SEAN *see his father dead, sees* HAYLEY *alive and realises what his brother has done.*

He takes the knife out of BLAKE*'s stomach. Blood pours onto the floor.*

BLAKE, *close to death, kisses* SEAN *gently on the lips*.

BLAKE. Now leave, love.

BLAKE *dies*.

Terrified, HAYLEY *runs to the front door, scrambles to open the last lock, opens it and exits fast leaving the door open.*

SEAN *lowers* BLAKE *to the floor. He places the knife down on the coffee table. His hand shaking, he takes a drink from a can of beer. He then looks towards the open front door.*

Reaching under the armchair he takes up the biscuit tin and opens it. He looks inside and takes out a handful of cash. He stands and puts the cash in his pocket.

He looks at the tape recorder in front of him. He rewinds the tape. He presses the tape recorder and 'An Irish Lullaby' begins to play.

He walks to the front door and stops just inside the flat.

He stands there for some time looking out.

He then closes the door and begins to lock it.

He faces back into the flat.

Now quickly and with purpose. SEAN *resets the coffins, lager, chicken.*

We watch him quickly move through the main events of the first act. DINNY *and* PADDY*'s entrance,* VERA *and* MAUREEN*'s entrance, the cheese and crackers on the plate, himself being struck by the frying pan,* JACK *and* PETER*'s entrance,* DINNY *fainting, and finally the Monopoly money being thrown into the air. This all lasts two minutes.*

SEAN *fires a look towards the front door.*

He walks out to the sitting room.

He picks up HAYLEY*'s coat and puts it on, he lifts up her bag and places it on his shoulder. He takes a plastic Tesco bag from the ground and holds it.*

He turns his back to us as he stands at the door. He's applying something to his face.

'An Irish Lullaby' comes to an end.

Silence.

SEAN *turns. He's covered his face in* DINNY*'s brown shoe polish. He's making* HAYLEY*'s entrance.*

Loud guttural rhythmic music fades up and fills the stage and auditorium.

The light eventually fades down on SEAN *as we watch him calmly lose himself in a new story.*

Blackout.

Silence.

Curtain falls.

The End.

The Walworth Farce was commissioned by The Druid Theatre and received its premiere at the Town Hall Theatre in Galway, Ireland, on March 20, 2006, with Denis Conway as Dinny, Garrett Lombard as Blake, Aaron Monaghan as Sean and Syan Blake as Hayley. It was directed by Mikel Murfi, designed by Sabine Dargent, with lighting by Paul Keogan. This production was also performed at the Everyman Palace Theatre in Cork, and the Helix in Dublin.

On August 2, 2007, the production opened at the Traverse Theatre in Edinburgh, Scotland, as part of the 2007 Edinburgh Festival Fringe, with Tadhg Murphy and Natalie Best taking over the roles of Sean and Hayley, respectively. It made its American premiere at St. Ann's Warehouse in Brooklyn, New York, on April 17, 2008, with Mercy Ojelade taking over the role of Hayley. This production was also presented at the National Theatre in London, and the Project Arts Centre in Dublin.